## ELITE SERIES

### EDITOR: MARTIN WINDROW

# The Crusades and the Crusader States

*Text by* DAVID NICOLLE Ph.D.

*Colour plates by* RICHARD HOOK

OSPREY PUBLISHING

Published in 1988 by
Osprey Publishing Ltd
Member company of the George Philip Group
12–14 Long Acre, London WC2E 9LP
© Copyright 1988 Osprey Publishing Ltd

*British Library Cataloguing in Publication Data*

Nicolle, David
   The crusades.—(Osprey elite; v. 19).
   1. Crusades, 1095–1274
   I. Title    II. Hook, Richard
   909.07

   ISBN 0-85045-854-4

Filmset in Great Britain
Printed through Bookbuilders Ltd, Hong Kong

**Dedication**
For my Dad, a founding father.

**Artist's note**
Readers may care to note that the original paintings
from which the colour plates in this book were
prepared are available for private sale. All
reproduction copyright whatsoever is retained by the
publisher. All enquiries should be addressed to:
   Scorpio Gallery
   50 High Street,
   Battle,
   Sussex TN33 0EN
The publishers regret that they can enter into no
correspondence upon this matter.

# The Crusades and the Crusader States

## Introduction

The Crusades seemed to erupt into the late 11th century Middle East without warning. Yet in fact they were the culmination of a century during which Catholic Western Christendom had been changing at an increasing rate—not least in its attitudes to war and religion. The 11th century also saw considerable economic growth and, though there were ups and downs, it would be wrong to see the First Crusade as a product of poverty, despair and resulting religious hysteria. Hysteria there may have been, but this did not create the Crusade.

In early Christian times warfare had been seen as evil, or at least unfortunate. Now, however, the concept of Holy War—of the *Vexillum Sancti Petri* Holy Banner given by the Church, of the *Militia Christi*, or of priests blessing a knight's sword became widespread, as did a growing cult of warrior saints like Michael and George; men who fell fighting for the Church now died as martyrs. Whether these ideas owed anything to the influence of Islamic concepts of *jihad* is hotly debated, but co-existence with Islam was now denied; Christ's enemies must be defeated and truth was to be proved by the sword.

In Spain and Sicily the clash between the Faiths was direct, but in the eastern Mediterranean things were more complicated. Here the Orthodox Church had faced Islam in a moderately tolerant atmosphere for centuries. Byzantium's struggle with the Muslims was more political than religious, and the confrontation had been complicated by the existence of huge Christian communities within many Muslim-ruled regions. Most had been under Islam for so long that they had more in common with their Muslim neighbours than with Western European Christians. Yet it was these people, as well as the Holy Places themselves, that the Crusaders were exhorted to liberate.

While Byzantium had plenty of experience of

The Laqlaq Tower forms the north-eastern corner of the Old City of Jerusalem. The city walls were rebuilt following the Ottoman conquest but much of this tower consists of medieval Mamluk masonry; it was just west of here that a section of the Crusader army under Godfrey de Bouillon broke into the Holy City.

Western mercenaries, who had long fought in Byzantine ranks (see Elite 9, *The Normans*), many ex-mercenaries had returned to the West together with veterans of less publicised mercenary service in Muslim armies. Such 'Franks', as Western warriors were known in the Middle East, were no longer ignorant of Middle Eastern warfare; yet such knowledge was restricted to sections of the military élite rather than being widespread among the bulk of Crusaders.

The ordinary people had been stirred to religious enthusiasm by a whole series of 'signs', in addition to the preaching of the Crusade itself. Meteor showers were seen in France; there were lunar eclipses and the moon turned blood red; marks were seen on the sun; a comet was recorded in autumn 1097, and a spectacular *aurora borealis* was interpreted as a religious manifestation.

In some parts of Europe this led to persecution of all who held different religious opinions, above all the Jews. Such activity was condemned by the Church and was often an excuse for mere extortion. Elsewhere it led to enforced conversion, and to what has been called the 'First Holocaust'. Could these events, or the massacre of Jews following the Crusader capture of Jerusalem, have prompted the conversion to Judaism of a certain Norman knight in 1102? He took the name of Obadyah the Proselyte and toured much of the Middle East in search of the Messiah. Elsewhere reaction against the persecution of Jews led to Emich of Leiningen, the leading Rhineland culprit, being consigned to Hell according to Christian legend following his death in 1117.

Nor were the Jews the only sufferers. In the Balkans certain 'heretics' of upper Macedonia were slaughtered by Crusaders from southern Italy. These were probably Bogomils (see Men-at-Arms 195, *Hungary and the Fall of Eastern Europe*) and their misfortune seems to have brought the wrath of their

*Demon shooting a broad-headed arrow from a composite bow; carved capital from ruined Crusader church, late 12th century. (Nazareth Museum, Israel)*

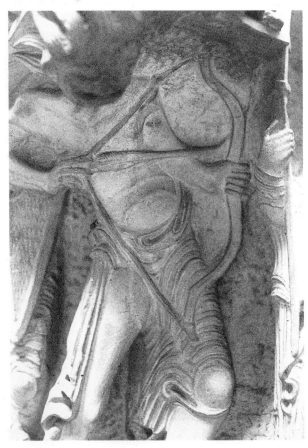

Pecheneg Turkish allies down on the Crusader column.

While in Europe the Crusaders persecuted non-Christians, in the Middle East they made few efforts to convert their foes. Perhaps the military respect they soon learned for the Turks also influenced their religious outlook, though dying Muslims were baptised on the field of battle in an act of macabre mercy.

Yet the seemingly miraculous successes of the First Crusade did lead to expanding ambitions. At first the Crusaders' task was to 'liberate' the Holy Places from Muslim control, but even before this was achieved the invaders began to see their rôle as the expansion of Christendom. Once Jerusalem was won, advocates of the Crusade began to think in terms of destroying Islamic civilisation in its very heartland. Meanwhile Muslim reaction developed from a mixture of local horror amid widespread apathy to an attitude of defensive *jihad*, and finally to the all-conquering ambitions of the Ottoman Empire.

# The First Crusade

The armies which marched east at the end of the 11th century represented a wide spectrum of the West European military establishment, as well as other sections of society. But not all European countries were equally represented. The First Crusaders mostly came from France, western Germany, what are now the Benelux countries and the Norman states of southern Italy. Nor was Europe homogenous in terms of military organisation. Northern France and Norman Italy were feudalised with a class of *miles* or knights having already emerged as a social as well as a military élite. A similar process was seen in southern France and Flanders; but as yet the concept of knighthood had made little progress in Germany, while in many parts of Italy 'communal' urban militias already played a vital military rôle.

The European background to the First Crusade (1096–9) is well known, as is the progress of the Crusade itself (see *Further Reading*), but even today the circumstances which the Crusaders actually found in the Middle East are not widely understood. The chronic disunity which characterised Islam at this time was seen not only in the Fertile Crescent, where Turkish Seljuqs and their successors, plus Egyptian Fatimids and various minor Arab dynasties struggled for control, but also in Anatolia. Here the victorious Seljuqs and Danishmandids had virtually driven out the Byzantines and were now squabbling over their spoils. In Iran and Iraq the Great Seljuqs were in rapid decline, while the Fatimid Caliphate of Egypt, having just recovered from a series of civil wars, was no longer the power it once had been. Syria and Palestine, the very targets of the Crusader assault, were a kaleidoscope of tiny autonomous city-states in most of which the Turks now formed a ruling military élite. Until very recently Armenian rulers had maintained a precarious independence in Antioch and Edessa (modern Urfa) while others still did so in the Taurus Mountains to the north. Some upland towns may even have remained nominally part of the Byzantine Empire; and the existence of all such enclaves probably owed much to their rôle as pawns in the wider struggle between Turk and Arab. Even though Edessa had lost its independence by the time the First Crusade arrived, the area was still dominated by an Armenian military élite and was relatively stable compared to neighbouring regions. Its towns had effective militias and dominated the surrounding countryside. Against such a background it is not surprising to find Armenians playing a prominent rôle in the armies of the subsequent Crusader States.

There is also evidence that the Turkish military élite of professional *ghulams* or *mamluks* had allowed their martial skills to decline, perhaps as a result of becoming involved in politics as the Seljuq Empire fragmented. Archery tactics which had previously driven Byzantine armies from the field were soon to fail against Crusader forces no better equipped than their predecessors. The Crusaders were able to meet their foes in close combat and to ride them down. What had changed? Crusader mail was no more proof against arrows than that of the Byzantines and, unlike many Byzantine and Middle Eastern troopers, these Westerners as yet made no use of horse armour. Perhaps the Turks, having neglected their training, were simply no longer able to shoot fast enough. It would, in fact, be more than another century before a Muslim army succeeded in halting a Crusader cavalry charge by arrows alone.

Woaira castle near Petra, Jordan. This 12th century fortification was known as *Vaux Moïse*, and consists of a walled rock surrounded by deep crevasses. The photograph shows an outer gate formed of a pierced rock which is now linked to the main castle (top right) by a modern stone bridge replacing a lost wooden structure.

Further south, in Palestine, the First Crusade met Fatimid armies which had much in common with those of Byzantium and Mediterranean Europe. Their cavalry élite was probably as heavily armoured as that of the Crusaders, while their weapons technology may have been more advanced. The Fatimids had, in fact, only retaken Jerusalem from the Turks a few months before the Crusaders appeared, and it has been suggested that part of the previous Turkish garrison remained in Fatimid service. To these were added Fatimid troops, some of Sudanese origin, and an *ahdath* local militia which included Muslims and Jews. *Ahdath* militias also played a leading rôle in the defence of the Fatimid coastal cities in Lebanon and Palestine—the last of which, Asqalon, held out until 1153.

The first Crusader armies to set out were not, in fact, official. These were the so-called Peasants' Crusades. Crusading was, however, an expensive business, and relatively few of the very poorest took part. The Pope himself emphasised the need for material preparation and the settlement of one's affairs before leaving home. Most who set out were moderately well-off, yet their actions were unwelcome to a Church and aristocracy which did not control such expeditions. Nevertheless most were led by knights and included many professional warriors within their ranks.

The first group set out under Walter the Penniless and maintained relatively good discipline. The

*Arrest of Jesus*; carved marble tympanum from Larnaca, Cyprus, 1200–1250, showing soldiers in full mail hauberks and chausses. The workmanship shows considerable Byzantine influence. (Victoria & Albert Museum, no. A2-1982, London)

Crusaders was basically a matter of survival. Many still starved to death, particularly in Anatolia and during the siege of Antioch. The 'poor', whose epic struggle rarely touched the chronicler's pen, were probably a more influential force than is generally recognised—even if only as a grumbling menace in the background. Their impatience with their leaders' quarrels boiled over in northern Syria during the winter of 1098–9, forcing the nobles to renew their march on Jerusalem. It was around this time that a semi-legendary Norman knight known as the 'king of the Tafurs' emerged from the twilight. The Tafurs seem to have been a particularly fanatical group of destitute Crusaders who would expel from their ranks anyone obtaining money. Their tendency to slaughter and rape, and their perhaps mythical habit of eating dead Turks during the Antioch famine, turned the Tafurs into a legend, while their 'king' became a major figure in later literary epics.

The upper ranks of the First Crusade included men like the Italo-Norman Tancred, who knew Arabic, while others had served in Byzantium, against the Muslims of Sicily or in Spain. The overall size of the army is unknown, but has been estimated at 30,000 infantry and up to 4,500 horsemen outside Nicea (Iznik) in 1097, plus non-combatants. Appalling losses during the march across Anatolia reduced the fighting strength to some 12,000 outside Jerusalem in 1099, of whom no more than 1,300 were knights. Losses in horses were even greater, so that the number of cavalry in Syria may have been as low as one or two hundred by June 1098, with other men fighting on mules. Not surprisingly, every effort was made to capture remounts in the horse-raising regions of northern Syria. Much arms and armour had also been abandoned on the march, yet this ragged army still fought under the banners of both great lords and *minores* (lesser leaders), some of which were already recognised by the Muslim foe.

One of the most remarkable features of these early Crusades was the speed with which they marched across Europe and the Middle East; Geoffrey de Bouillon's force averaged 15.5 miles per day in 89 days, of which 59 were actually on the road. Peter the Hermit's Peasants' Crusade achieved 17.7 miles per day in 103 days, of which 86 were on the march. Smaller groups of horsemen

next, under Peter the Hermit and Fulk, were more disorderly, though Peter's army did reach Constantinople. A fourth expedition under Gottschalk was well equipped and apparently disciplined, but suffered from the reputation of those who had gone before; it was destroyed by the Hungarians. The fifth and final Peasants' Crusade, though large and led by members of the nobility, behaved badly in Germany, tried to besiege a Hungarian frontier city and was similarly wiped out. Those who did reach Turkish territory were annihilated because their cohesion had evaporated, this in turn probably resulting from the exhaustion of money with which to purchase food. Militarily they were also unable to deal with the tactics and discipline of their Turkish foes.

Plenty of the 'poor' marched with the official First Crusade, and many other participants plumbed the depths of poverty before reaching Jerusalem. The prospects of material gain were in fact so dim and the risks so huge that there remained little scope for purely material motives. The obsession with money and loot shown by so many could make 20 to 25 miles per day for a limited period, while some of the huge later armies had a line of march three days long. Naturally there were desertions, but late-comers joined the column and troops could also be picked up along the way. A certain Hugh Bunel even turned up during the siege of Jerusalem, having wandered the Middle East for 20 years after committing a murder in his native France. Many Normans, Danes, Frenchmen and Anglo-Saxons had served in Byzantium's south-eastern frontier garrisons less than a generation earlier and many stayed on to fight for both Armenians and Turks, while 'Franks' of unclear Western origin served in Fatimid Egypt well into the 12th century.

As if the First Crusade did not face enough problems, it soon quarrelled with the Byzantines. A tide of anti-Byzantine sentiment among the rank and file was unwelcome to the leadership, who realised that they still needed the Byzantine Empire for supplies, for overland communications, and because it remained, despite recent reverses, the major Christian power of the Middle East. In the event the Crusaders captured and held Antioch without Byzantine help in a series of episodes which were at the time regarded as miraculous. Quarrels over the city's future simply exacerbated a divided leadership. The discovery of the supposed Holy Lance may have come at a convenient moment to reunite the ranks, but such miracles were commonly believed and should not be seen in too cynical a light.

The conquest of Jerusalem by the First Crusade has probably been analysed more than any other Crusader battle, yet questions remain and new evidence is still coming to light. It now seems that not all the Christians were driven out as potential 'fifth columnists' by the Fatimid garrison, and surviving letters in the Cairo Geniza (synagogue documents store) show that the Crusaders did not quite exterminate the remaining non-Christian inhabitants. As is well known, part of the garrison surrendered as prisoners of war. Some Christians may have been found sheltering in the Church of the Holy Sepulchre and the surviving Jews were forced to clean the bodies of slain Crusaders before fleeing to Fatimid-held Asqalon along with the ransomed garrison. Other unransomed prisoners

**The upper caves at 'Ain Habis, Jordan, showing a niche-like oratory containing a carved cross. Known as the *Caves de Suet*, these formed the most famous 'cave fortress' in the 12th century Crusader States (see Plate L).**

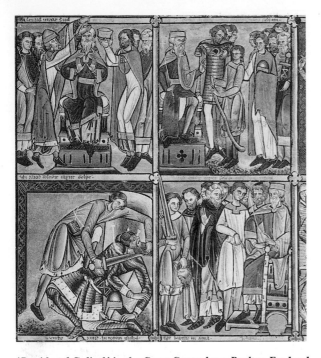

*'David and Goliath'* in the *Great Canterbury Psalter*, **England 1180–90, showing the kind of equipment used by King Richard's army on the 3rd Crusade. (Bib. Nat., Ms. Lat. 8846 f.2v, Paris)**

were later slaughtered, although a few survived by turning Christian. Jerusalem had been captured and recaptured many times during previous inter-Muslim conflicts, but had never seen such slaughter, and the savagery of the 'Frankish' Western Christians sent shock waves throughout the region. On the other hand the Crusaders do not appear to have indulged in the ritualised and partly symbolic rape of female captives which had been a feature of previous wars. Nor were they ignorant of the value of their loot, many books later being ransomed for considerable sums of money.

# Establishment of the Crusader States

Despite the fear and outrage there was no real understanding of Crusader motivation, and few saw the invasion as a threat to Islam. Even the Muslim recapture of Edessa in 1144 was more political than religious in inspiration, and this gave the Crusaders much-needed time to consolidate their hold on Palestine and parts of Syria. Their position

remained very vulnerable, as the majority of Crusaders had gone home after conquering the Holy City which, together with Ramla and Haifa, was now guarded by no more than 300 knights. A shortage of war-horses was even more acute as ships were as yet unable to transport animals direct from Europe. Capturing horses from neighbouring territory became a military priority.

Next came the need to repopulate Jerusalem itself; yet the Crusader Kingdom never managed to make the city anything more than a political and religious centre. Empty and half-ruined, Jerusalem was home to a few hundred Europeans, too few even to garrison the city's gates. The surviving local Christians seem to have fled, and neither Jews nor Muslims were permitted to return. But after campaigning in what is now east Jordan, King Baldwin I encouraged the area's indigenous Christian population to migrate to Jerusalem, where they settled around the Church of Mary Magdalene on the north side of the empty city. Baldwin II encouraged a few more European settlers, while the kingdom's simple and almost military court began adopting the trappings of oriental splendour.

Down on the coast Italian fleets from Genoa, Pisa and Venice soon arrived, and it was due to their efforts that the coastal ports were gradually conquered. Such aid was repaid with commercial concessions which were later to cost the kingdom dear. Only Asqalon held out under its Fatimid garrison, and even their raiding was inhibited by a surrounding chain of castles. In the semi-desert regions of southern Palestine and eastern Jordan (Oultre-Jourdain) Crusaders and Arab Bedouin came to terms. The latter remained a potent military force but preferred to be left alone. Relations with the settled Arab villagers were less satisfactory, the peasantry often leaving their fields uncultivated rather than pay taxes to the invader.

Elsewhere things progressed in different ways. Tancred led only a handful of knights plus 500 foot-soldiers north from Galilee when he took over control of Antioch in 1101; but by May 1104 he could field an army of maybe 3,000 cavalry and 7,000 infantry. Here in the north the newly formed Crusader states of Antioch and Edessa soon clashed with Byzantium over the overlordship of Antioch itself, as well as control of Latakia and domination of Cilicia. At times the Crusaders found themselves allied with the Armenians and at others fighting against them. Meanwhile the Crusaders made great efforts not only to recruit the Armenians but to settle them within the Crusader States. Some Armenian mercenaries may have transferred their allegiance from the Fatimids to the 'Franks', and large numbers of this warlike people clearly did fight beside the Crusaders, as either allies or mercenaries; yet the relationship remained cautious. The Crusader States also got drawn into the tangled politics of Anatolia and northern Syria. At one time the County of Edessa even joined a Muslim leader against an army from the Principality of Antioch allied to a second Muslim faction.

Great help might have been expected from Europe following the conquest of Jerusalem, and in fact the Crusades of 1101, which were never graced with a number, came as a direct response to the astonishing success of the First Crusade. They set out in high confidence, highly motivated and well equipped, but proved disastrous. At the time their failure was put down to arrogance, pride and other sinfulness. The fact that they appeared to march off into the wilderness of eastern Anatolia, perhaps aiming for Iraq and Baghdad, would be a measure of the sublime over-confidence that gripped Western Christendom in the wake of the First

*Demon spanning an early form of crossbow*, **late 11th century carved capital. (*in situ* Cathedral of St. Sernin, Toulouse)**

**Antique, probably Roman pillars re-used in the medieval sea-walls of Asqalon and photographed in 1918. These gave lateral strength on a sandy subsoil, but are now exposed because the sea walls have largely eroded away. (IWM photo, London)**

Crusade. In reality these Crusades faced an entirely new strategic situation, for this time the Turkish rulers of Anatolia were co-operating with each other. As a result no further Crusader armies successfully took the overland route to the Holy Land.

While the remaining Crusaders were struggling to establish and expand their states in the Holy Land, the military situation was also changing in Europe. The 12th century was a period of considerable development in military organisation and even tactics, though the most dramatic advances in arms and armour had to await the late 13th and 14th centuries.

France was the fountainhead of what has come to be known as the 12th Century Renaissance, as well as being the source of most military developments. With increasing professionalisation, mercenary cavalry soon played a vital rôle, and by the early 13th century an army could include equal numbers of knights and mounted sergeants, numerous crossbowmen (some of whom operated as highly mobile mounted infantry), and other professional infantry armed with a variety of weapons. Yet there remained a widespread prejudice against any form of missile weapon—crossbow, simple bow, javelin or sling. A knight generally would not use such devices in war, and certainly not against other knights. Richard the Lion-Heart's love of the crossbow was, in fact, considered shocking. This did not mean that feudal warfare was bloodless; but to kill a fellow knight invited a blood feud as well as losing a ransom. It was even foolish to harm his horse, for such valuable *destriers* were well worth capturing.

Germany was even slower to accept the necessity of missile weapons. The whole German Empire (First Reich or 'the Empire' as it was generally known) was, however, renowned for its infantry and Byzantine recruiting masters regarded even the German knightly class as better on foot with swords than the French, who were famed with lances on horseback. Even the concept of knighthood had been slow to appear in Germany, not really developing until the reign of Conrad III. The Crusades and Military Orders may also have influenced this development.

In Italy the situation was again different and possibly more relevant to developments within the Crusader States. Although the rural areas were feudalised, in the cities militias already played a dominant military rôle. These included non-noble but fully armoured cavalry, while the bulk of the infantry seems to have come from the surrounding *contado*. Such northern Italian armies were noted for better discipline than most other 12th and 13th century forces, as well as having greater ability to co-ordinate the actions of horse and foot. Yet by the 13th century professionals were again numerous. Italy had exported mercenary marines and sailors from at least the 11th century, and they were followed in the 13th century, by highly paid crossbowmen. In the deep south, in the Norman kingdom, the situation was again different (see Elite 9, *The Normans*). This highly feudalised but also Byzantine- and Islamic-influenced area played a leading part in the history of the Crusades. Contact with the Crusader States remained close (though not always friendly) under the subsequent Hohenstauffen and Angevin dynasties.

**Sahyun Castle in the coastal mountains of Syria, the biggest of the Crusaders' 12th century constructions. It was defended by a huge man-made ditch (right), a keep and upper citadel (centre), while an older Arab-Byzantine fortress stood within the central castle (far left). (Syrian Dept. of Antiquities & Museums)**

# The Later Crusades

**'David and Goliath' in an English manuscript from Winchester, 1150–75. (Pierpont Morgan Lib., Ms. 619v, New York)**

Although the Crusading efforts of 1101 ended in disaster this merely made the First Crusade seem more miraculous and thus divinely ordained. Confidence was undimmed, and the Crusader States continued to expand. Changes within the neighbouring Muslim areas were not understood, so when the vulnerable County of Edessa fell to Zangi of Mosul in 1144 a shock was felt throughout Europe. There had been bloody defeats before, but this time the Crusader States were clearly in retreat. A Second Crusade (1147–8) was summoned in response—and ended in humiliating failure beneath the walls of Damascus. Once again defeat was blamed on sin. In reality the entire strategic situation had changed, though as yet the Muslims remained too divided to follow up such successes. Throughout the Middle East there was a revival of Islamic *Sunni* orthodoxy aimed against not only the invading Crusaders but also the 'heretical' *Shi'a* branch of Islam, which had long threatened *Sunni* dominance. Not until the mid- and later 12th century, under Nur al Din and Saladin, did a consequent revival of *jihad* have much impact on the battlefield; but from the Fall of Edessa onward the

Crusaders were on the defensive—though not always realising it themselves. A breathing space was allowed under Saladin's immediate successors, who preferred detente with the Crusader States, but the coming of the Mamluks in 1250 meant that *jihad* was again in the ascendant. The Crusader States now had less than half a century to live.

Another effect of the disastrous Second Crusade was to make Europe aware of Muslim might. In response to the supposed 'pride' of those who had failed came a revival of 'humility' among later Crusaders, at least in terms of dress, undecorated military equipment, moderate eating and sexual abstinence. This may have been good for discipline, but it occasionally led to friction with a military élite in the Crusader States who had adopted many seemingly soft and 'oriental' habits. In reality acceptance of Middle Eastern costume, cuisine and domestic arrangement made sense given the area's climate and cultural heritage.

Military arrogance was harder to deal with. Subsequent European Crusader forces consistently spurned the aid and advice of locals. A greater strategic awareness was, however, developing. The Church made strenuous though unsuccessful efforts

11

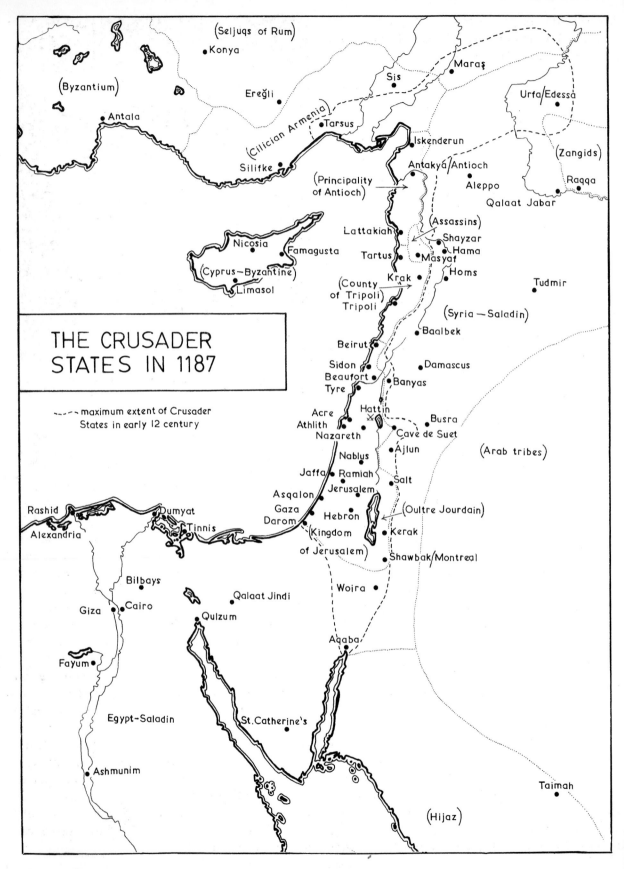

THE CRUSADER
STATES IN 1187

---- maximum extent of Crusader
States in early 12 century

(Seljuqs of Rum)
Konya
Maraş
Sis
Ereğli
Urfa/Edessa
(Byzantium)
Antala
(Cilician Armenia)
Tarsus
Iskenderun
(Zangids)
Silifke
Antakya/Antioch
Raqqa
(Principality
of Antioch)
Aleppo
Qalaat Jabar
Lattakiah
(Assassins)
Shayzar
Nicosia
Famagusta
Tartus
Hama
Masyaf
(Cyprus—Byzantine)
Krak
Homs
Tudmir
Limasol
(County
of Tripoli)
Tripoli
(Syria — Saladin)
Baalbek
Beirut
Sidon
Damascus
Beaufort
Tyre
Banyas
Acre
Hattin
Busra
Athlith
Cave de Suet
Nazareth
Ajlun
(Arab tribes)
Nablus
Jaffa
Ramlah
Salt
Jerusalem
Asqalon
Gaza
(Oultre Jourdain)
Darom
Hebron
Kerak
Rashid
Dumyat
(Kingdom
Alexandria
Tinnis
of Jerusalem)
Shawbak/Montreal
Bilbays
Woira
Qalaat Jindi
Giza
Cairo
Qulzum
Fayum
Aqaba
Egypt-Saladin
St.Catherine's
Ashmunim
Taimah
(Hijaz)

to ban trade in military goods with Muslim ports. Attitudes towards the Crusade also changed, with many people suggesting that the sword was not the best way to confront the challenge of Islam. Another phenomenon which even today is widely unrecognised was the large number of Christian warriors who either served as mercenaries in Muslim or Mongol armies or turned renegade after capture. They included men whose lands were overrun following Saladin's victory at Hattin in 1187, and even ex-members of the Military Orders. In 1223 the Patriarch of Alexandria claimed that there were no less than 10,000 renegades in Muslim service; and a Spanish Templar is said to have commanded forces in Damascus in 1229. In 1250 the French Crusader De Joinville met a fellow countryman from Provins who had come to Egypt with a previous expedition, turned renegade and become a rich man.

A more positive development was the appearance of transport ships capable of carrying horses directly from southern Europe to Palestine, providing a lifeline for the Crusader States. By the late 12th century it was possible for armies like that of Richard I of England to arrive fully equipped and ready for battle. Richard I's Crusade was, in fact, notably well prepared, even to the extent of bringing 50,000 spare horse-shoes manufactured in the Forest of Dean. The English monarch was the first European king to lead his own fleet to the East and in so doing he set a high standard for those who followed.

Despite Richard's admirable preparations, his victories on the field and his high reputation among his Saracen foes, the Third Crusade (1189–92) was only a qualified success. Even so it stands head and shoulders above the rest, many of which were diverted from their original destinations. The Second Crusade had been intended to rescue Edessa. Its German contingent tried to go overland through Turkish Anatolia and was virtually wiped out. Even those contingents which reached the Middle East were diverted against Damascus, an ally from whose walls they were humiliatingly repulsed. The Third Crusade is harder to evaluate. Most of the Crusader States had been lost to Saladin after his victory at Hattin, and this Crusade was intended to win back at least the city of Jerusalem. In this it failed. Jerusalem was not regained, but the

*The scourging of Christ*, **late 11th–early 12th century carved capital showing the equipment used in southern France. (*in situ* church, St. Nectaire)**

Crusader States were revived. Even Richard's seizure of Byzantine Cyprus provided the Crusaders with another kingdom and a useful base.

The Fourth Crusade (1202–4) was the most catastrophic diversion of all, though its official target of Egypt was never quite clear. Instead it conquered Constantinople, and dealt the Byzantine Empire a wound which in the longer term proved to be deadly. Above all it guaranteed that Catholic and Orthodox—Western and Eastern—Christianity could never again co-operate in real trust against their Muslim foes. The Fifth Crusade (1218–21) aimed at Egypt and was not diverted, but failed after initial success led to arrogance, an unwillingness to compromise and eventually to utter defeat. The Sixth Crusade, (1228–9) was a remarkable success but, by regaining the Holy Places of a demilitarised Jerusalem by compromise and diplomacy, led to the disgrace of its leader. The Seventh Crusade (1248–54) repeated in extraordinary detail the aims, errors and results of the Fifth. Louis IX's Eighth Crusade to Tunisia in 1270 was another clear diversion of effort, though perhaps with some strategic sense. Yet it too ended in military catastrophe.

# The Crusader States

The fortified town of Qalaat al Mudiq. Known as *Famya*, it formed the southern outpost of the Principality of Antioch and was a Hospitaller 'commandery'. The existing walls largely date from the 13th century.

While later Crusading expeditions generally failed, the survival of the Crusader States themselves was quite remarkable. Their problems were numerous and to some extent self-imposed. The near-miraculous success of the First Crusade left the Crusaders believing that they were surrounded by weak, fragmented foes and that the entire Middle East was an open frontier. Within a very few years this was, of course, no longer the case. Yet the need to conquer more land and military fiefs was essential for the proper development of a feudal society. This the Crusaders failed to do, largely because they lacked the manpower. The one 'open area' that they did win, the County of Edessa, was soon lost and none of the other great inland cities— Damascus, Homs, Hama, Aleppo, Diyarbakr or Mosul—ever fell. This left the Crusader States as a coastal strip concentrated around the ancient ports but with insufficient land to support a large feudal army. Great opportunities opened up for trade and urban expansion, but the conquerors were mentally unprepared for such a future, which was left to the Italian merchant colonies to exploit.

In fact the late 11th century feudal system which, with its associated attitudes, they brought from Western Europe had evolved in a situation of military manpower surplus and weak monarchies. The Crusaders now found themselves in a situation

of acute manpower shortage and with a need for effective central government. Their states were slow to respond to such unfamiliar circumstances, and although the power of the major barons was fragmented in the mid-12th century, that of the king also soon declined. At a time of military crisis the military élite resisted changes which were essential to survival. The Kingdom of Jerusalem developed, in fact, a passion for writing laws to confirm a conservative, increasingly unreal and essentially 'colonial' feudal structure. To the very end the Crusader States remained torn between an increasing need to co-exist with powerful Muslim

Carved capital of 1087–1119. The warriors in this carving have been interpreted as Crusaders or as 'warrior monks' but their lack of visible mail hauberks may simply be a local southern French fashion. (*in situ* Cloisters of Ste. Foy, Conques)

neighbours and a persistent urge to conquer. This urge had been inherited from their early days and was constantly reinforced by Crusades from the West.

The organisation of the Court in Jerusalem was based on that of France. Four major offices of state were the *senechal*, *connetable*, *marechal* and *chambellan*. The first was primarily concerned with ceremonial and justice, though its holder also inspected castles in the king's name, organised their supplies and changed their garrisons. *Chatelains* (castle commanders) answered only to the king. In war the *senechal* fought alongside the ruler in the royal division or *bataille*. It was the *connetable* (*regni constabularius*) who actually commanded the army under the king, as well as taking military command and presiding over the High Court in the latter's absence. The *marechal* (*regius marescalus*) assisted the *connetable*, organising the army, paying the mercenaries and holding regular reviews to check on equipment and discipline. He was also responsible for horses and pack animals, in turn being helped by the *grand turcopolier* who commanded the royal *turcopoles*. The *chambellan* was primarily concerned with the king's personal well-being; while a fifth, non-military, high office was that of *chancelier*.

## Fiefs and Salaries

Even in war, however, the king was often no more than first among equals, his leadership depending upon personality. The king also had to pay for a knight's horse and equipment when campaigning beyond the frontiers, promising to replace lost animals in a form of insurance called *restor*. Furthermore the king was obliged to protect a knight's fief against enemy raids or invasion. On the other hand the military obligations placed upon fief-holders were much heavier than those in most of Europe where, in fact, they generally declined during the 12th and 13th centuries. A man could be summoned for an unlimited period, though a knight was theoretically excused from fighting on foot in defence of a castle or town. Members of the military élite were also involved in war at an early age, less than 15 years, though it should be remembered that their sisters were bearing children when as young as 13. Most sources say that a man could be called upon until he was 40, though in some cases a warrior seemed to serve until 60.

Generally speaking war was seen as a youthful occupation, with great emphasis being laid on the ardour and enthusiasm of the inexperienced *bacheler* in the popular tales of the time. On the other side it is worth noting that some Muslim authors maintained that warfare demanded experience and prudence, and that 40 was the warrior's optimum age.

## Local troops

Few non-knightly cavalry are recorded in the early 12th century, but the service of *servientes loricati* (armoured servants) and *serjens a cheval* (mounted sergeants) become more common later in the century. Not that all the knightly class were of European origin—most of those who settled after the First Crusade married local women and produced a class of so-called *poulains*. These were

*'Camilla and Turnus besiege Montalbanus'* in the *Eneide* of Henrik van Veldeke, a manuscript of the late 12th–early 13th century showing typical German military styles. (Deutsche Staatsbib., Ms. Germ 20282, f.46v, Berlin; Bildarchiv Foto Marburg)

soon integrated as a vital part of the military élite. Though Catholic in faith, the *poulains* often clung to aspects of local culture and were sometimes despised by the supposedly 'pure blooded' Westerners. Other warriors of direct Middle Eastern origin, including some Armenians, were also raised to knighthood in the 12th century, while all the cavalry except the Turcopoles fought together. Nevertheless, grades of military status remained rigid to the end. An agreement on compensation for deaths outside official warfare, reached between the Lady Isabella of Beirut and Sultan Baybars of Egypt in 1269, stipulated that a captive knight be released in compensation for a slain knight, a Turcopole for a Turcopole, footsoldier for footsoldier, peasant for peasant.

The system of fiefs which supported this feudal élite was particularly complicated. Not only was the number of fiefs inadequate, but men owed service to more than one lord. Some fiefs were held by women, while others were Church fiefs which might owe no military service at all. The earlier Muslim *iqtas* had been similarly small and fragmented, though the relationship between Crusader fiefs and the preceding system of military land-holding has not been fully studied. Most feudal lords were, like their Muslim predecessors, absentee landlords drawing rents from their property but living in a neighbouring town. This was unlike the feudal system of, for example, 12th century France, where

the lord was a vital member of the local community, and it reinforced the great gulf between indigenous Arab inhabitants and their new masters. Consequently there are few fortified manors on the map of the Crusader East. Those that do exist seem more like watch-towers and fortified barns in which the lord's land-agent could store the produce of his much-raided estates. Other smaller fiefs were held by non-noble sergeants and Turcopoles.

The entire system was disrupted in 1187 when so much Crusader territory fell to Saladin. Though some ground was regained following the Third Crusade there seems to have been no more nonnoble fiefs, while even a member of the aristocracy now had to be dubbed a knight before taking over his estates. The 'Frankish' peasantry, never numerous, disappeared into the cities or turned renegade, so that the inhabitants of the countryside were now wholly indigenous. One solution to the shortage of land was to create the *fief de soudée* or money-fief for the many landless men and pilgrims who came to the East. These were not paid directly by the government but were the tolls of ports, markets, mills and bridges. Such fief-holders were, of course, city dwellers and their military obligations were unlimited. The origins of the idea are obscure but some Muslim *iqtas* were similarly based on tolls and dues. An increasing number of knightly and even lordly families had to rely on such sources of income after the disaster of Hattin, until by the last years of the Crusader States the great majority of fief-holders had such *fiefs de soudées*.

The military and political organisation of other

*Virtues and Vices*, **French carving of c.1185 showing smaller kite-shaped shields, long guiges and pointed helmets. (*in situ* west portal of church, Aulnay-de-Saintonge)**

Crusader States was similar to that of the Kingdom of Jerusalem. These owed theoretical, but not often effective, allegiance to Jerusalem, and in 1186 Saladin even thought it worthwhile offering Muslim 'knights, sergeants and crossbowmen' to Count Raymond III of Tripoli in the hope of encouraging his defection. Mercenaries were commonplace in the armies of all Crusader states. Such men included knights who held no fiefs; instead they were paid salaries for as long as they were needed—or as long as the ruler could afford them. Others were paid by lords and fief-holders to serve in place of perhaps no longer existing lesser vassals. Rich and powerful men also maintained their own mercenary forces, particularly in the last anarchic years of the Crusader States.

In addition to these Westernised troops were those of local origin who fought in traditional ways. The most famous were the Turcopoles who were distinct from the many native-born sergeants. Known personal names suggest that in the early days many were converted Muslim prisoners of war, of whom there were a large number. Such Turcopoles fought as light cavalry, usually as horse-archers though not using the highly mobile harassment techniques of the nomadic Turks. Rather they operated like the professional *mamluks* or *ghulams* who formed the core of most Islamic armies. Many later Turcopoles may have been descended from these converts and the great majority were soon placed under the control of the Military Orders.

**Kerak castle in southern Jordan with the fortified hilltop town on the right. Most of the existing fortifications were built by Paganus the Butler in the 12th century.**

Other local troops also played a significant rôle, particularly in the 13th century, though the religious and social gulf between them and the dominant 'Frankish' Catholic élite remained wide. The Maronite Christians of Lebanon were among the most effective, particularly as light cavalry and as infantry archers in mountain warfare. The *Shi'a* Muslims (Alawites and Nusayris) of the Syrian coastal mountains were equally effective, but were unpredictable to both Crusader and *Sunni* Muslim paymasters. They reserved their most reliable support for the *Shi'ite* Muslim Ismailis (Assassins) of the same mountainous region. For much of the 13th century the coastal range remained largely outside the control of both the coastal Crusader strip and the Muslim inland cities, some of its *jabaliya* (hill-folk) inhabitants supporting one side, some the other.

**Military Orders**

In contrast the Crusader Military Orders were totally dedicated to the triumph of the Cross, though this did not stop them from clashing with those who ruled the Crusader States. These Orders soon provided the largest and most effective standing armies in the Crusader East, and by the 13th century the Orders of the Temple, Hospital and Teutonic Knights were essential not only in offensive operations but for garrisoning the main

**The keep at the southern end of the upper bailey of Kerak castle. This part of the complex was extensively rebuilt after Saladin captured the castle.**

Crusader castles. They came to see themselves as the real guardians of the Holy Land, though there remained deep antagonism between the Temple and the Hospital. Their history is well known (see MAA 155, *The Knights of Christ*) though their origins are obscured by legend.

The immediate reason for the creation of the Templars was a danger from Muslim raiders and local peasants who picked off unwary pilgrims on the road to Jerusalem in the early 12th century. The Order was finalised in 1128, and from then on its Brothers were full-time fully committed members of a monastic order whose patently military character was justified by the need to defend the Church. Little is known about the training of *novices* or young members but it appears to have been informal. The *novitiate* system was, in fact, soon abandoned, and men joined as adults already trained in the military arts. Far less attention was placed on education than in the ordinary monastic orders, so that Templars often regarded themselves as *simplices* (unlearned) in religious matters. Rules on behaviour, celibacy, personal property and military discipline were extremely strict. Privacy was unknown, diet was frugal, washing infrequent and sports forbidden. A man often slept in his ordinary clothes, prayed frequently and owed total obedience to his superior. The organisation of the Temple mirrored that of the kingdom itself, with its own *maitre*, *senechal*, *marechal*, supervisor of uniforms and regional commanders. Such commanders had their own quartermasters, under-marshals and standard-bearers. Both Temple and Hospital also had naval leaders, the Hospitaller *amiral* and the Templar *grand commandeur de la mer*. Those who fell in battle were regarded as martyrs, and the Hospitallers developed a whole mystique of martyrdom.

### Militias

Another important source of troops were the militias. Real urban communes did not appear until after the battle of Hattin in 1187, that of Tyre being a short-lived early example which evolved in the dark days of 1187–88 when this city was virtually the last outpost of the Kingdom of Jerusalem. Earlier militias were simply urban forces, some perhaps organised around local fraternities, rather than representing a true commune. Nor were they very important until the 13th century. By then some coastal cities were expanding fast as refugees flooded in from the shrinking Crusader hinterland. Acre was a prime example, with the growth of a new walled suburb of Montmusard. Nevertheless Acre did not have a recognised commune until 1232, and Tripoli as late as 1287, although Antioch's commune had been legitimised in 1193. Long before the recognition of such communes urban confraternities or brotherhoods played a military rôle, forming individual units within the militia, each under its own banner. Most members were settlers of European origin, though the confraternity of Sts. George and Belian was for local Syrian Christians. The bourgeois of such cities already defended their walls and provided the ruler with units of both mounted and infantry sergeants; again, these had to be paid if serving beyond their own area. Generally speaking, however, urban forces were loyal to local leaders rather than to the king and this could be another source of weakness. The rôle of the city-based nobility in such communes is hard to determine, though it might have been considerable. Cities could certainly provide disaffected members of the nobility with great wealth and fortified bases from which to defy the ruler.

In general the military situation of the 13th century Crusader enclaves had much in common with the great cities of medieval Italy, where there was a comparable urbanisation of the military aristocracy. Within the coastal cities there were also influential and increasingly independent Italian merchant communities. They similarly provided forces for the defence of the city as well as frequently fighting among themselves—Genoese against Venetian against Pisan. Smaller Italian cities also had such Middle Eastern colonies which were similarly liable for military service, that of Ancona in Acre being obliged to provide 50 fully equipped soldiers, *armes de fer au meins*, when needed.

In the 12th century the Crusader States were sometimes able to field formidable forces. The County of Edessa could only maintain 100 knights but never had a chance to develop its full potential. Rich Antioch could call upon some 700 knights, smaller Tripoli from 200 to 300 and the relatively large Kingdom of Jerusalem about 1,000. These figures represent, of course, the situation before the battle of Hattin. A proportion of ten infantry to one horseman seemed normal in Tripoli and was

*David and Goliath*, **southern French relief carving c.1145 showing scale armour and the inside of a shield. The scale hauberk may reflect garbled accounts of Muslim lamellar armour.** (*in situ* **façade of church, St. Giles du Gard**)

probably similar elsewhere. More than 10,000 assorted non-noble troops were thus maintained by the Crusader States, the Church and the cities. To these could be added the Turcopoles, the increasingly important Military Orders and passing pilgrims from Europe.

**Outlying possessions**

After the Fourth Crusade had conquered Byzantine Constantinople a similar 'colonial' form of feudalism was imposed upon Greece and, for a while, European Turkey. Many men, including Turcopoles and Syrian Christians, left the threatened Crusader States in Syria and Palestine for what looked like the greener pastures of the Latin 'Empire of Romanie'. Here military obligations were not the same as in the Holy Land, but were heavy enough. The *Assises de Romanie* showed that military service was owed until the age of 61. Thereafter a man's obligation could be undertaken by his son, another knight or two squires. Even in peacetime he had to serve four months of every year in a castle garrison, four on the frontier and the rest at home.

The situation was similar in the Crusader Kingdom of Cyprus. The population of this island was remarkably mixed, though the overwhelming majority were still Greek-speaking Orthodox Christians. Remnants of an earlier Arab-Islamic occupation seem doubtful, but there were certainly Arabic or Aramaic-speaking Syrian Christians and Maronites as well as Armenian military colonies on

Probably *David and a Philistine*, carved capital of *c.*1120. Such scenes would be based on concepts of Crusading warfare against the Saracens. (*in situ* nave of Cathedral, Vezelay)

Cyprus before Richard I conquered the island at the end of the 12th century. Most of the subsequent settlers were of European origin, and they formed a tiny ruling minority. Most lived in towns alongside merchant communities from Italy, southern France and Catalonia. Their numbers increased dramatically as the other Crusader States crumbled in the second half of the 13th century, the refugees including mixed-origin *poulains*, Armenians and Syrian Christians. In the early days the army of Crusader Cyprus included 300 enfiefed knights and a much larger number of mounted sergeants, as well as urban militias from five fortified cities. Turcopoles are similarly recorded in Cyprus, some being given their own *fiefs de turcopoles*. As in the Holy Land, a military aristocracy rarely lived on its estates. In Cyprus, however, the main military threat came from the sea, and a number of splendid coastal fortresses were built. The Military Orders took a leading rôle in this process, introducing the concept of concentric castles—such as that at Paphos, which has so much in common with Belvoir in southern Galilee.

The Crusader States also maintained a small fleet, that of the County of Tripoli having been created after an Egyptian squadron forced an entry into Tolosa harbour in 1180. Local ships previously supported the 1168 invasion of Egypt and the Kingdom of Jerusalem also maintained some galleys at Tyre. Despite a considerable orientalisation of the Crusader military élite there was a clear determination to keep 'Franks' and locals distinct, with laws forbidding natives from wearing European costume. Crusader warriors reportedly also regarded it as 'dishonourable' to wear the Muslim military coat or fur *tarbush* hat. Generally speaking it was, in fact, Armenian and Byzantine styles that the Crusaders adopted rather than those of their Muslim foes.

## Allies

The Armenians were the most important of the Crusaders' regional allies—as distinct from local troops recruited within the Crusader States. Many Armenian mercenaries became available in the early 12th century as fewer of them went to serve in Fatimid forces. Numbers of such troops were also floating around Syria in the chaotic early Crusader period, fighting for all and sundry. Those on the Christian side served as both allies and mercenaries, as cavalry and as highly regarded infantry archers, sometimes in large units under their own princes. At times their numbers reached 4,000 horsemen and 10,000 infantry. The feudalisation of neighbouring Cilician Armenia in the late 12th and early 13th centuries made it even easier for Armenian warriors to fit into the armies of the Crusader States. The important rôle played by Cilician Armenia in the military history of the Crusaders has rarely been recognised, though it was well understood by both Crusaders and their Muslim foes. Meanwhile the inability of 'Franks' and Armenians to overcome their cultural and political differences was a major source of weakness.

Interior of Shawbak castle. Known as *Crac de Montreale*, this fortress was largely built by Paganus the Butler; it resisted a siege of a year and a half before falling to Saladin after the battle of Hattin. Like Kerak it was also greatly strengthened by the Mamluks.

Another important Christian power was Georgia. Though not a direct neighbour of the Crusader States it played a significant regional rôle. Georgian troops fought as infantry and as armoured cavalry, some using javelins or bows. Their armour and equipment was very similar to those of neighbouring Islamic armies (see MAA 171, *Saladin and the Saracens*). Similar to the Georgians and closely allied with them was the Byzantine 'Empire' of Trebizond (Trabzon). Its relations with the Crusader States in Syria were tenuous, but it came into frequent, though not always friendly, contact with the Crusader 'Empire of Romanie' following the Fourth Crusade. Trebizond's cavalry, probably armoured in normal Byzantine style, fought with lances, while the infantry of its mountainous hinterland were noted archers with composite bows. Mercenaries from the Crusader States served all these Christian powers. Men from Antioch were, in fact, prominent throughout Anatolia in both Christian and Seljuq-Turkish armies. Others fought for Byzantium, playing a leading rôle in the tragic battle of Myriokephalon in 1176. Others had helped a Byzantine invasion of Egypt some years earlier. Fewer seem to be recorded after the Mongol invasions of the mid-13th century, though men who had either moved on from the Crusader 'Empire of Romanie' or who had failed to find a place in Crusader Greece fought for the Byzantines against that same Crusader 'Empire'.

# Collapse

The collapse of the Crusader States in the late 13th century was a culmination of a long decline, the growing strength of Muslim foes and various other factors. With the benefit of hindsight some of their actions seem suicidal, but those who ruled the Crusader States were neither stupid nor particularly wicked.

The feudal structure inevitably changed as Crusader territory shrank. Most of the land around a great city like Tyre was now held by the king or the Venetians, most of the aristocracy having only money fiefs. The military obligations of all fiefs naturally remained paramount, but those of the coastal cities were relatively more important. The feudal nobility now held very few castles and many were poverty-stricken, living in the faded grandeur of their city houses. Earthquakes, droughts and

**'The Army of Holofernes before the city of Bethulia'** from the Apocryphal Book of Judith in the *Arsenal Bible*. This unusual manuscript was made in Crusader Acre late in the 13th century. It illustrates Islamic-style costume with remarkable accuracy, but the armour worn by these soldiers is neither Crusader nor Muslim. It may, therefore, portray Byzantine or Armenian styles. (Bib. de l'Arsenal ms. 5211, f.252, Paris)

*Arrest of Jesus*, **late 13th century French carved capital showing a soldier with a mail coif and a winged or flanged mace of Islamic inspiration.** (*in situ* **Cloisters of St. Trophime, Arles**)

*Arrest of Jesus*, **early 13th century French carved capital showing an earlier soldier wearing full mail and helmet with a low comb across the top.** (*in situ* **Cloisters of St. Trophime, Arles**)

locust plagues had devastated the region and the constant need to pay ransoms ruined many families. Though the king, prince or count still held much land, such rulers had lost considerable power to the Military Orders. These Orders also held their territories in *frankalmoign* or freehold, which meant that they owed no direct feudal dues to the crown. They were, however, obliged to defend not only their great frontier castles but also certain sections of city walls.

The Crusader States invited further hostility from the warlike Mamluks of Egypt by co-operating with the Mongols against these Mamluks. The latter had taken over from the relatively easy-going Ayyubid successors of Saladin in 1250, and they were eventually to snuff out the last Crusader remnants. At the time, however, many believed that the Mongols might not only defeat the Mamluks but overrun the entire Muslim Middle East, and they were seen as valuable allies. Yet it

was not to be: the Mamluks drove back the Mongols who themselves soon became Muslim. At the same time European piracy against the Egyptian coast, often stemming from Crusader Cyprus, prompted reprisals by sea and land. This, and two previous Crusades aimed specifically against Egypt, led the Mamluks to adopt a scorched earth policy as the Palestine and Syrian coasts gradually fell to their assaults. They hoped thus to deny bases or supplies to any further Crusader naval landings. Crusader fleets, including those that escaped from places like Tripoli before it fell to the Mamluks, kept up the struggle for some time, and the Mamluks responded by building war-fleets with which to menace Cyprus. On land persistent Mamluk raids led to the sharing of revenues from an already much reduced Christian territory. At the same time Mamluk siege skills reached a high degree of sophistication, perhaps even including the use of primitive forms of gunpowder.

Yet even the fall of the last coastal cities like Antioch in 1268, Tripoli in 1289, Acre, Tyre, Sidon, Beirut, Haifa, Tartus and Athlit all in 1291, was not quite the end. Templars clung to the small off-shore island of Arwad for another 12 years. The Frankish élite of Tripoli remained under Mamluk suzerainty for several years, perhaps as late as 1302; so did the Genoese of Jbeil, before being evacuated to Cyprus. Elsewhere the military aristocracy was either wiped out or made its escape by sea, while those of the poorer classes who survived rapidly merged with the native Christian population.

# Strategy, Tactics & Organisation

The numbers of Crusader troops involved in various battles are not known. Contemporary chronicles are unreliable, but scholars have made estimates based upon these and other evidence. The Belgian military historian J. F. Verbruggen worked out the following table:

| Date | Battle | Knights | Infantry |
|------|--------|---------|----------|
| 1098 | Antioch lake | 700 | ? |
| 1098 | Antioch | 500–600 | ? |
| 1099 | Asqalon | 1,200 | 9,000 |
| 1101 | 1st Ramla | 260 | 900 |
| 1102 | 2nd Ramla | 200 | ? |
| 1102 | Jaffa | 200 | ? |
| 1105 | 3rd Ramla | 700 | 2,000 |
| 1119 | Athareb | 700 | 3,000 |
| 1119 | Hab | 700 | ? |
| 1125 | Hazarth | 1,100 | 2,000 |

One limiting factor on the size of all Middle Eastern armies was the availability of pasture for raising horses. Northern Syria was better off than the south, which gave the County of Edessa and the Principality of Antioch an advantage over the Kingdom of Jerusalem. It gave an equal advantage to the Muslim states of the northern zone, though only in the maintenance of professional cavalry, since Turkish tribal forces needed far more mounts for their horse-archery tactics. In fact the similarity which was soon seen between the armies of the

Crusader States and those of Byzantium probably reflected a common response to common problems rather than direct Byzantine influence.

Apart from the use of slightly more sophisticated tactics there was very little military development in the Crusader East. Greater caution could lead to misunderstandings with newly arrived Crusading armies from Europe, while there was also a clear appreciation of wider strategy. Even Reynald of Châtillon's apparently wild campaigns into Arabia and the Red Sea coast in the 1180s may have been designed to divert Saladin's attention away from Aleppo and to damage his prestige as guardian of the Muslim Holy Places. If so, then they succeeded—for a while.

In battlefield terms the Crusader States learned from their allies and from their enemies. Drums may have been used to maintain order, while the Templars sometimes used bells as a summons to arms. Banners placed in wagons as rallying points for urban militias probably reflected Italian influence.

Much more important, and again similar to developments in Italy, was the degree of co-ordination achieved between cavalry and infantry in the Crusader States. This must have reflected the threat from a largely mounted foe. In the 12th century it was still normal for infantry to precede cavalry during an advance, opening their ranks when the horsemen charged. This was the same system as that of the Fatimid Egyptian army. When

'Nimrud and his soldiers' in a *Histoire Universelle* made in Acre *c.*1286. **This manuscript again shows an interesting mixture of Western and Byzantine styles plus, perhaps, a transitional form of armour between the Islamic *jawshan* and the European coat-of-plates. (Brit. Lib., Ms. Add. 15268, f.71r, London)**

The castle of Birecik, photographed in 1918. This large fortress overlooks a crossing of the River Euphrates on the road between Antioch and Edessa (Urfa) and formed a vital point in the defence of these Crusades States. (IWM photo)

mounted armies, though these were generally small raiding forces such as those involved in cattle rustling around Edessa in the first half of the 12th century. Most such troops would have worn light armour and may have copied some of the traditional light cavalry skills of the Middle Eastern horseman, though not, of course, his horse-archery. Small Crusader units sometimes copied the Islamic practice of mounting an infantryman on a horseman's crupper for additional mobility. Real mounted infantry also accompanied some raiding forces, and were certainly used to intercept caravans between Egypt and Syria in the semi-desert regions of southern Jordan and southern Palestine. Warfare in these desert areas was, however, generally confined to winter and early spring when pasture was available.

True cavalry was of course the primary offensive arm in Crusader armies. The tactical rôle of the Crusader knight was the same as that of his cousin in Western Europe—namely to break through enemy ranks by weight and momentum, though not much speed, and then to turn to strike them in the rear.

on the march in open country armoured infantry formed a defensive box around the mounted knights, the rôle of crossbowmen being particularly important in keeping enemy cavalry at bay. Whether Crusader infantry were able to attack enemy horsemen in the flank or rear—as they were trained to do in Europe—seems doubtful except perhaps in rugged terrain. The failure of these defensive infantry tactics often led to defeat, whereas successful co-operation between knights and crossbowmen, as in the siege of Acre during the Third Crusade, generally led to victory. Even during offensive manoeuvres the infantry normally covered the cavalry's initial advance. This in-evitably made Crusader forces cumbersome when compared to those of their Turkish enemies. Muslim forces, other than those of the Fatimids, generally placed cavalry ahead of the infantry when on the march. It was presumably their influence that led the armies of the later Crusader States to form up cavalry outside the defensive infantry box—into which the riders could still retire at need.

Of course, the Crusader States also used wholly

Carved quatrefoil showing perhaps a *Virtue* armed in typical mid-13th century French style, c.1230. (*in situ* west front of Cathedral, Amiens)

Flank attacks were attempted whether the foe was mounted or on foot. The power of the close-packed unit of heavily armoured knights was largely psychological, and this might account for their rapid decline following the appearance of disciplined infantry who could no longer be frightened into breaking ranks. The frequent success of knights riding up a beach directly from their ships also perhaps resulted from this psychological impact, while the development of specialised landing ships in the late 12th century obviously contributed to this capability. In contrast only the Byzantines and Muslims seemed able to use cavalry defensively to harass and disrupt an enemy attack.

Generally speaking the cavalry of the Crusader States seem to have fought in smaller groups than that of Europe and to have learned the technique of repeated small-scale attacks rather than one massed charge. The use of reserves for flank attacks, ambushes and tactical support was seen in the West, but was highly developed in the Crusader States even by the early 12th century. Whole sections of an army could use hills as cover in the hope of luring forward a foe. Such a large unit would probably consist of a *bataille*, which in turn consisted of

**Qalaat Faraun photographed by T. E. Lawrence in 1917. This fortress stands on a small island, known to the Crusaders as the *Isle du Graye*, off the coast of Sinai south of Aqaba. It has never been properly explored, but most of the fortifications appear to date from the Crusader period. On the other hand Aqaba was walled in the Fatimid period, so the foundations of Qalaat Faraun may also be pre-12th century. (IWM photo)**

smaller *conrois*. The *conrois* was drawn up in one or more very closely packed ranks with heavily armoured knights in front, lighter sergeants behind and squires in the rear. Such social distinctions were a relatively recent phenomenon for in most parts of Europe the *miles* or knight only evolved into a 'nobleman', rather than simply a warrior, early in the 12th century. Distinctions were accentuated by the rapidly rising cost of full cavalry equipment, with sergeants soon having to be supported by knights or lords. In the 12th century this led to the gradual disappearance of unarmoured cavalry from the *conrois*, while in the 13th century there was a rapid decline in the proportion of fully armoured knights to lighter sergeants and squires; this sank to one to ten by the early 14th century.

Even by the time of the First Crusade the identity of a *conrois* was probably indicated by pre-heraldic patterns on its shields. Each *conrois* consisted of 20 to

**Possibly *The Siege of Jerusalem by the First Crusade* on an early 12th century carved relief. The men attacking from the left wear mail hauberks (A), while those attacking from the right wear mail and lamellar (B). (*in situ* north door church of San Nicola, Bari)**

40 men divided into smaller *echelles* (squadrons) or *compagnie* (companies). All would train together, the earlier *Causa Exercitii* manoeuvres evolving into the classic 13th century tournament. Emphasis was placed not only on individual skill at arms, but also on an ability to operate as a team with iron discipline and loyalty to one's comrades. This latter was shown in various episodes recorded in Crusader chronicles. For example, the new high-peaked saddle and long stirrup leathers, which were associated with use of the couched lance, also meant that it was difficult for a man to remount if unhorsed. On such occasions his comrades would form up around him, protecting him until he was safely back in the saddle. Men would also stick together if more than one lost his horse. Other tactics reflecting the special conditions of Crusader warfare included efforts to attack a horse-archer on his more vulnerable right side, and trying to strike horse-archers if they dismounted to shoot more accurately.

The true high saddle had become almost universal among European knights by 1100, and a century later had also developed hip-hugging *arcons* on the cantle, plus a more protective pommel. A knight's spurs were similar to those of the Greeks and Romans, except that they developed a curved outline to fit around the ankle bone; but a major change came with the adoption of the rowel spur, which probably resulted from the use of larger horses. This rowel spur was not, however, common until the 14th century. Interestingly enough, the Egyptian Mamluks adopted gilded spurs in the late 13th century as a badge of the Sultan's own fief-holders, almost certainly in direct imitation of European knightly spurs.

Outside the European tradition of most Crusader cavalry were the Turcopoles. They were sometimes described as 'the archers of the Franks', but this can be misleading as Turcopoles also acted as light cavalry without bows and arrows. Nor did they use the high speed harassment techniques of Turkish tribal horse-archers. They had, in fact, a great deal in common with the cavalry of both Byzantium and professional Islamic armies. Many appear to have been converted prisoners-of-war, which would account for the fact that Turcopoles were almost invariably executed if recaptured by the Muslims. Their name actually means 'sons of Turks', and in other respects their recruitment mirrored the practice of both Byzantines and Seljuks among the mixed populations of the Greek-Turkish Anatolian frontier. Many years later Turcopoles were of mixed European and indigenous parentage, while others may have been recruited from the indigenous Christian population. Though their armour was much lighter than that of the knights they often fought alongside Crusader heavy cavalry, particularly that of the Military Orders, under whose authority most 13th century Turcopoles were found. Turcopoles and mounted crossbow-armed infantry also served in the armies of the Latin 'Empire of Romanie' following the Fourth Crusade and were prominent in Cyprus after this island was conquered by the Third Crusade.

As mentioned above, the infantry of the Crusader States played a vital rôle. Spears, often used as pikes, were the basic defensive weapon while bow and crossbow kept the enemy at a distance. Adding bows of composite (wood, sinew, horn and/or bone) construction to the basic crossbow was a major technical advance in the late 11th and early 12th centuries. Composite bows had probably never been abandoned in southern France and Italy since Roman times and Provençal infantry clearly used crossbows during the First Crusade. When fighting in defensive ranks behind the spearman, a crossbowman often had more than one weapon plus a loader to achieve a higher shooting rate. The Crusaders did not, however, introduce the crossbow to the Middle East. Fatimid forces already used this weapon to a small degree, while the infantry of Syria and northern Iraq had adopted it at least by the 12th century. Even Byzantine crossbows seem to be recorded in 12th century Cyprus.

Paradoxically, it is possible that Crusader infantry learned new weapons from their too-often despised Fatimid foes. The infantry of Egypt apparently used long-hafted maces and other staff weapons with considerable success against Crusader horses in a manner similar to that seen later in 13th century France and 14th century Flanders. The infantry of the Crusader States were soon employing wooden barricades in open warfare, as did their foes, and there are even a few references to the use of siege engines in open battle. In the mountainous terrain of much Crusader territory Christian infantry tried to anchor their flanks on natural features like ravines, cliffs or steep hills, while light infantry archers and skirmishers could also cover these flanks. When such a tactic was not possible, infantry would adopt a rectangular or circular formation. The most typical Crusader footsoldier seems to have been heavily armoured, a long mail hauberk protecting his legs but also making him slow to manoeuvre. In the 13th century, however, Crusader infantry increasingly found themselves called upon to operate in the coastal mountains which now formed the frontier. Such troops became, according to their foes, adept in ambushes and fighting in the rugged terrain around such castles as Crac de Chevallier, Beaufort and Baghras.

Though infantry archers and crossbowmen were

*'Saul destroys Nahash'* in the *Maciejowski Bible*, **Paris c.1250. This magnificent manuscript illustrates a great variety of mid-13th century equipment including, as here, a man-powered mangonel. (Pierpont Morgan Lib., Ms. 638 f.23v, New York)**

more important in the 12th and 13th century Crusader States than in Western Europe, few lessons seem to have passed westwards as the result of experience of warfare in the Latin East. European archers had to prove their necessity all over again on the battlefields of 14th century Europe, and even then continued to use the finger-draw rather than the stronger thumb-draw of the East. The primitive longbow survived as a weapon of war in England and Scandinavia, and was even once recorded in 'Frankish' hands during the Third Crusade—probably used by an Englishman in the retinue of Richard the Lion-Heart. Weight for weight the composite bow had twice the power of such simple longbows and although the composite bow had long been known in Mediterranean Europe its further development, though not its continued use, was halted by the spread of the crossbow.

A field in which European warfare is more likely to have been influenced by both the Crusades and warfare in Spain is that of sword-play. Even by the 11th century European swordsmen were showing greater sophistication in their techniques, but as yet it was all cut and no thrust. Such a development probably accounted for the longer guards seen on late 11th and 12th century weapons. Contact between Islam and Europe via Italian trade also played a part and it is clear that the fencing style later known as 'Italian' had its origins in the East. In this a man placed his forefinger over the cross or quillons of his sword, thus obtaining greater control for both cut and thrust. Some scholars suggest that the adoption of a thrusting technique resulted from the spread of plate armour or early forms of coats-of-plates (see below); but it is just as likely that the coat-of-plates itself resulted from the threat of a thrusting sword. The history of arms and armour is full of such 'chicken and egg' scenarios, most of which boil down to the simultaneous spread of both chicken and egg, neither one nor the other taking clear chronological precedence. Meanwhile one of the earliest European fencing manuals, written for the education of the knightly class, appeared in Milan around 1295. The use of knives and daggers in battle is also testified in written sources before such weapons appeared in the idealised pictorial art of the 13th century.

# Castles and Siege Engines

When the Crusaders reached the Middle East at the close of the 11th century they found most of the towns and all the cities heavily fortified. In northern Syria and what is now south-central Turkey these defences were both strong and elaborate, while the region was also dotted with castles dating from the days when it formed a long-established frontier zone between Byzantium and Islam. The Crusaders also inherited the formidable defences of the Syrian-Palestinian coastal towns, since these too had been

**Hisn al Akrad in central Syria, the *Krak des Chevaliers* of the Crusaders. The central portion of this huge fortress is largely of 12th century construction, the rest mostly being added in the early 13th century when Krak was a major operational base for the Order of the Hospitallers.**

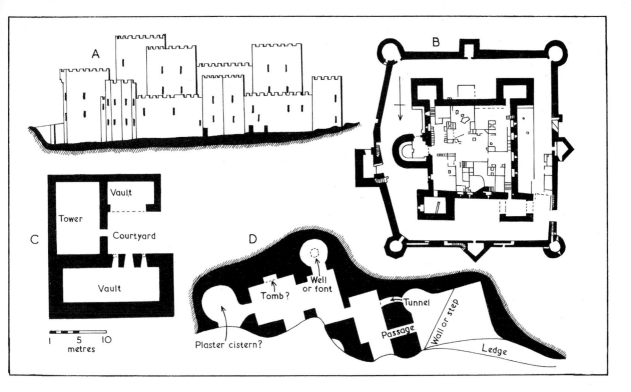

in the frontline of Byzantine-Muslim confrontation. The new-comers immediately repaired what they found, and it was only inland, in central Syria, Lebanon, Palestine and the east bank of Jordan, that the Crusaders had to start almost from scratch. The central part of what became the seigneury of Oultre-Jordain (north and south of Amman) was never, in fact, fully fortified as Crusader control was never complete. Only in the south of Jordan did mighty 12th century fortresses rise at Kerak, Shawbak, and on a smaller scale around Petra.

The whole question of castle-building, its relation to perceived military threats and the fertility of surrounding land is still not fully understood. These fortresses are huge both in numbers and often in size, yet they are not evenly spread. Earlier scholars assumed that their rôle was essentially defensive, to block invasion routes and to watch over vulnerable frontiers. For this reason, it was said, they were often built within sight of each other or were able to keep in contact via elaborate signal systems. Now, however, this view is regarded as oversimplified.

A castle is static and could not, before the age of cannon, actually 'block' any road. On the other hand a castle could serve as an operational base for both defensive and offensive forces. It also served as a place of refuge for a tiny ruling élite in case of

**(A) Reconstruction of the northern side of the *Castle of Forty Columns* at Paphos in Cyprus. This late 12th–early 13th century concentric castle was similar to that at Belvoir in Palestine and may similarly have been designed by the Hospitallers (after Megaw). (B) Plan of the *Castle of Forty Columns* at Paphos (after Rosser). (C) Plan of a building known as *al Babariyya* near Taiyiba in Palestine, which formed part of the fortified Crusader manor of *Forbelet* (after Benvenisti). (D) Internal plan of the upper-level caves at 'Ain Habis, the cave-fortress of *Caves de Suet*, based upon verbal descriptions and external photographs (after Nicolle).**

defeat or local uprising, as happened after the catastrophe at Hattin in 1187. Existing castles already served as administrative centres and this the Crusader castles continued to do, while the few European peasant settlers generally remained close to their walls. Elsewhere, as along the frontier with Damascus, remarkably few castles were built, whereas in the south a whole series of relatively small fortifications were soon erected around the Fatimid-held city of Asqalon. No doubt they inhibited raids by the Asqalon garrison, but they also enabled Crusader forces to threaten and blockade. When the evidence is weighed it appears that, at least in the expansionist period of the 12th century, most new or greatly enlarged Crusader castles were built as offensive bases close to areas where the conquerors hoped to expand or, as in the case of southern Jordan, close to a vital communications artery linking Egypt and Syria. The

Crusaders' failure to sever this artery is a feature of their military history which has received less attention than it deserves.

The first Crusader castles were relatively small and simple, the massive Syrian fortress of Sahyun being the only construction on a massive scale to be built during the early 12th century; even here the Crusader work was erected around an existing Byzantine-Arab fortress. A new feature for the Middle East was the introduction of European-style stone keeps as part of a larger structure. Most were lower than those in the West, being built entirely of stone in a region short of timber. Such keeps were placed at the most vulnerable part of the defences, although in flatter terrain they could stand at the centre of the complex. This may have contributed to the further development of the concentric castle, although concentric fortifications without a keep or citadel were well known in Islamic architecture.

(A) Section through the castle of Montfort in Galilee, built for the Teutonic Knights in 1226-29. (B) Section through the Crusader keep at Safita (*Chastel Blanc*) in Syria. It formed a fortified church for the Templars, and still serves the local Christian community (after Tuulse). (C) The coastal *Pilgrim's Castle* at Athlith, south of Mount Carmel. Mostly dating from the 13th century, it had two harbours, the northern now having eroded away while the southern is partly silted up (after Johns). (D) The complicated entrance to the castle of Krak de Chevalliers in Syria (after Lawrence).

Not surprisingly, Byzantine military styles influenced Crusader designs, though not as much as some have claimed. Byzantium had traditionally relied on small castles with relatively large garrisons or on walled towns defended by abundant though ill-trained urban militias. The Crusaders faced a very different situation in which military manpower was desperately short but highly skilled. On the other hand the Crusaders did adopt the Byzantine rock-cut ditch to isolate a hilltop castle, taking the concept to extraordinary lengths—and depths. The Byzantines are also credited with teaching the newcomers about the *machicolis* or small overhanging chamber from which besiegers could be bombarded or shot at. Yet this idea was already widespread closer at hand, among the Armenians and the military engineers of Syria.

Armenian influence on Crusader fortification was probably more important than that of the

**Relief carving of German infantry warriors, 1130–40, carrying large round shields. (*in situ* exterior of Abbey Church of Andlau, Alsace)**

*Saul on the road to Damascus,* **carved font from Tournai, early 12th century clearly showing the high war-saddle associated with the use of the couched lance. (*in situ* Church of Our Lady, Dendermonde)**

Byzantines, the Armenians having already had a profound impact on defensive architecture in Syria, northern Iraq and even Egypt. Apart from sophisticated features like the *machicolis*, the Armenians also made subtle use of natural features in a mountainous land, and their military engineers, as well as garrison troops, were soon recorded in Crusader service.

From the Muslims the Crusaders took the bent gate-entrance, the sloping *talus* anti-mining device at the base of a castle wall and the re-use of antique columns laid horizontally to give lateral strength to a wall. The *portcullis* to strengthen a castle door was known to the Romans but may have been re-introduced to the Middle East by the Crusaders. There is also no doubt that the details of castle decoration, as well as some constructional features, were often purely French. In other castles, like that of Montfort, which was built by the Order of Teutonic Knights, German characteristics could be found.

A widespread use of siege engines also had its influence on castle design. Not all such engines were for attack and it has been suggested, though by no means proved, that some special forms of castle embrasure were designed to accommodate large frame-mounted crossbows. Much more important in the evolution of castle design was the invention of the counterweight *trebuchet*. Unlike earlier mangonels this machine could be operated by a small team, and was also much more accurate. It had a profound impact on the design of fortifications from the early 13th century onwards—not, as might be expected, because of its use by besiegers but because

**The great tower of the castle of Jbail, *Giblet* of the Crusaders. This is one of the best examples of a western-type stone keep set amid Middle Eastern forms of defence.**

of its rôle in defence. Castles and city walls were now built with more numerous, higher and more protruding towers which served as artillery emplacements for these new counterweight *trebuchets*. Such engines could bombard the more exposed attacking forces, provide enfilading fire in case of an assault and, most important of all, made counter-bombardment of the besiegers' machines extremely effective. Crusader chronicles were soon full of descriptions of the power and accuracy of such devices, particularly in the hands of defending Muslim garrisons—for it is clear that Islamic siege engineering was still in advance of that of the Crusaders. The struggle for Acre during the Third Crusade is only one example and only a few years later, in 1204, the Fourth Crusade suffered similarly at the hands of engines defending the walls of Constantinople. The limitations of defensive artillery are, however, highlighted by the fact that the Crusaders eventually succeeded in both these hard-fought sieges. By the late 13th century it also seems clear that Western European *trebuchets*, and other siege engines, were just as advanced and complicated as those of the Middle East.

In the early days the Crusaders prevailed by sheer dedication and ferocity. The First Crusaders, when they besieged Jerusalem, used man-powered mangonels to hurl blocks of marble from demolished building, and shot fire-arrows into the bales of straw with which the defenders sought to protect their walls from such stones. Seven years later Afamea on the River Orontes was successfully blockaded by the excavation of a ditch around the entire fortifications—though this might be a chronicler's exaggeration. In 1111 Tancred's men formed their shields into a roof or *testudo*, as Roman legionaries had done, in order to force their way through a breach in the walls of Azaz. A more advanced technique was the movable wooden siege-tower. This had been used in the siege of Jerusalem and, together with the ram, remained more popular among the Crusaders than their Muslim foes; the latter preferred mining and the use of massed mangonels. The mobile siege tower seems, in fact, to have been abandoned in the Middle East after the collapse of the Crusader States in the late 13th century. Both sides used fire-arrows or large crossbow bolts with red-hot points to burn an enemy's wooden siege equipment. Both also stationed armoured infantry to protect such engines from sorties by the defenders, while a besieger's own camp was sometimes also protected by elaborate field fortifications.

Specialists in the design, construction and operation of siege engines, as well as military architects, were highly regarded and well paid in the Crusader States. Many came from neighbour-

See text for caption.

A

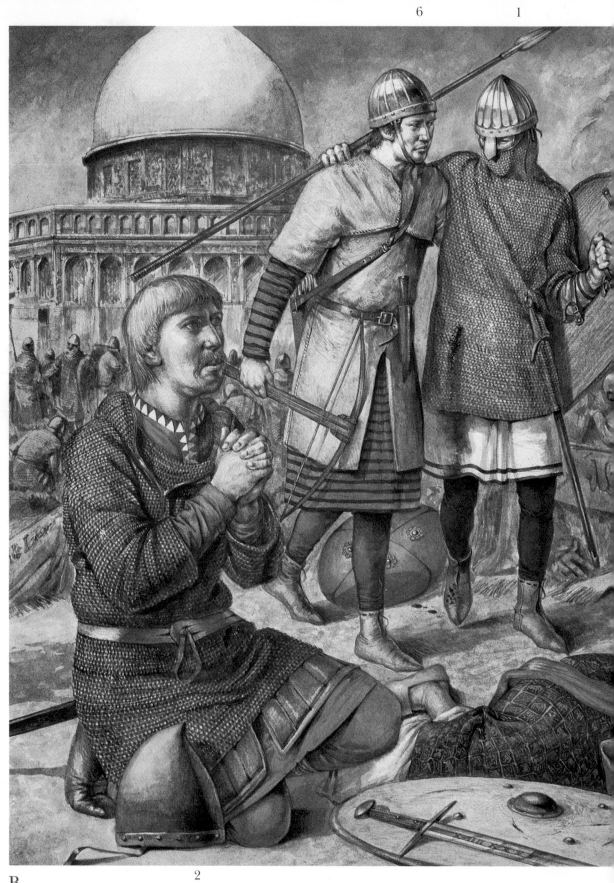

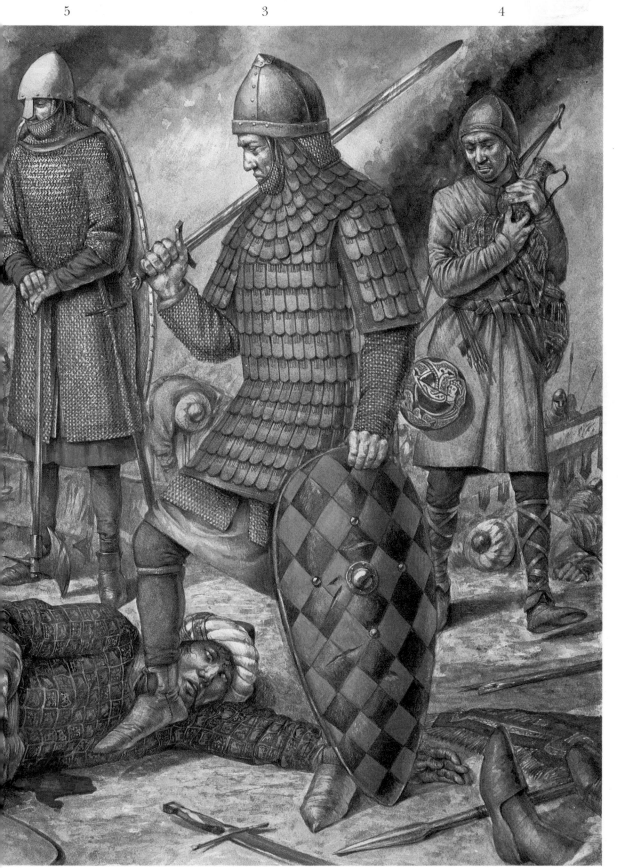

See text for caption.

D          3          See text for caption.

1

3　　　　　See text for caption.　　　　　2

E

F

See text for caption

1          3     See text for caption.     2        **G**

1

2

3

See text for caption.

2

1  3  See text for caption.  I

J      2             3     See text for caption.     1

2          See text for caption.     1

K

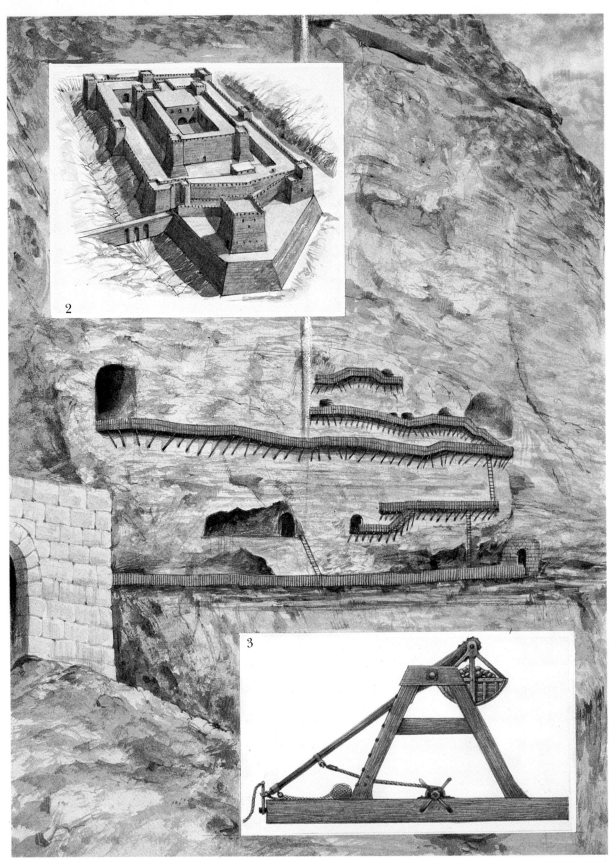

See text for caption.

ing Armenian areas, and the various traditions of engineering are reflected in the names given, particularly by Muslim authors, to different types of stone-throwing device. As mentioned above, the counterweight *trebuchet* was almost certainly invented in the eastern Mediterranean, probably within the Muslim area. The 'Frankish' or 'Rumi' (European) type was one of the simplest. The name originally referred to a basic man-powered mangonel but, by the mid-13th century indicated a simple counterweight type. Despite the development of this and much more advanced forms of *trebuchet*, the old man-powered mangonels remained the most numerous stone-throwing devices throughout the Crusader era, probably because of their ease of construction, transportation and use. The next step was the invention, in the mid-13th century, of a *trebuchet* with an adjustable counterweight. Again the Muslims seem to have been more adept in the use of these highly accurate devices, though it is as yet unclear who invented the machine. Almost certainly of Islamic origin was a *trebuchet* modified to shoot bolts rather than boulders.

Another extraordinary and so far unexplained defensive device was a T-shaped arm designed to drop things on an attacking force. Perhaps such a machine is illustrated in the mid-13th century *Maciejowski Bible* from France. Here a T-shaped arm with a locking mechanism on the other end is used to hoist the dead King Saul above the walls of Bayt Shan. Rather less obscure, but still not fully understood, are a series of large crossbows, some apparently mounted on frames. Heavy though not frame-mounted siege and counter-siege crossbows also needed a team of loaders to help the man who actually pulled the trigger. Winches to span such large bows were known in 13th century Islam and may also have been used in the Crusader States, though they did not become widespread in Europe until the 14th century. Others had movable defensive screens mounted in front while still others were modified to shoot small containers of 'Greek Fire'.

The possibility that the Crusaders' Mamluk foes possessed a real but primitive form of gunpowder by the late 13th century remains a matter of intense controversy among historians of science. If they did so then the Crusader States, or rather some of those who survived their fall, may have played a part in the transmission of the 'secret' of gunpowder to

(A) Reconstruction of a man-powered mangonel. This 12th century version was operated by a team of up to 20 men. (B) The *ziyar* or 'skein bow' was one of the most powerful weapons of the Crusading era. This reconstruction is based on an illustrated description in a manuscript made for Saladin.

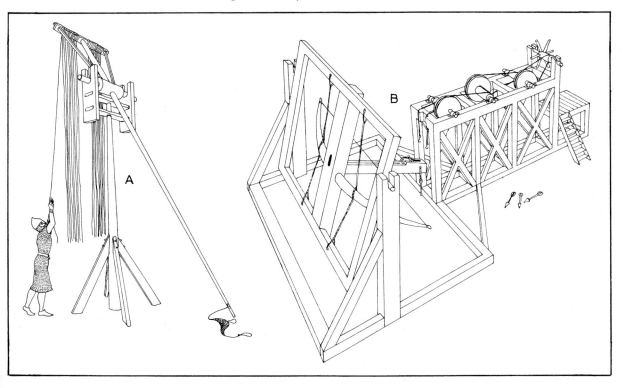

**Northern ramparts of Yilanlikale. This well preserved castle north-west of Antioch was one of the most important fortresses in Cilician Armenia and may have been partially built by the Hospitallers.**

early 14th century Europe. A possible candidate for such a rôle was Othon de Grandson, a Swiss who led a small band of English knights to the final desperate defence of Acre in 1291 and who later showed an interest in various exotic forms of weaponry.

At first the cost of constructing, garrisoning and maintaining castles had largely fallen to the king, count or prince. But the huge sums involved gradually led these rulers, particularly the King of Jerusalem, to cede more and more castles to the wealthy Templars, Hospitallers and Teutonic Knights. Though fortresses were still designed to be garrisoned by relatively few men, the cost and numbers could be considerable. The rebuilding of the castle of Safad after 1240 cost over one million 'Saracen bezants' during the first two and a half years' work, and thereafter about 40,000 bezants annually. Its peace-time garrison consisted of 1,700 men including 50 knights, 30 sergeants, 50

Turcopoles, 300 archers, 820 workmen and 400 slaves; in war this number rose to 2,200 souls. Such castles obviously needed huge stores of weapons, food and other supplies. Recent excavations at the Castle of Forty Columns in Crusader Cyprus unearthed huge numbers of crossbow boltheads and 1,500 stone balls for mangonels or *trebuchets*. Other more valuable military stores may have been recovered following the earthquake which destroyed this fortress.

Life in such castles was not, of course, entirely grim and militarised. Even the fortresses of the Military Orders could be decorated with wall paintings. Others had carvings, wall hangings and even mosaics. The life of those who inhabited such castles included hunting, music-making and the use of steam-baths in clear imitation of their sophisticated Arab neighbours. Castles also served as local industrial centres, some having mills for grain, olive oil or sugar cane.

The fall of these awe-inspiring fortresses might seem in need of explanation. Some gave way following prolonged sieges and near starvation, others suffered a collapse of morale and almost all seem to have been undermanned when it came to the final reckoning. Others were betrayed from within, and there was always the knowledge that too prolonged a resistance tended to be followed by a massacre. It would, in fact, probably be true to say that the reasons why these castles fell were as varied as the castles themselves.

# Arms & Armour

During the early medieval centuries Western Europe had, in general, been on the receiving end of Byzantine military fashion, while from the 12th century onwards the reverse was true. Yet in the Crusader States the situation was more complex. Here Byzantine styles may still have been seen, though both Byzantium and the Islamic world were at the same time under strong Turkish influence. So perhaps it would be fairer to say that Byzantines and Crusaders were both in receipt of Turkish fashions, while the Crusader States were also under the more direct influence of their non-Turkish or partly Turcified Muslim neighbours.

In general, however, the military equipment of the Crusader States mirrored that of western Europe. One of the best available sources is the *Rule of the Temple*, which described this Order's arms and armour in considerable detail. A ban on decorated harness, spurs or armaments was of course specific to the Military Orders, though a lack of conspicuous display was widely regarded as showing good intent. In the 13th century each Templar brother knight was to be equipped with a mail hauberk, mail chausses, a helmet or *chapel-de-fer* war-hat, sword, shield, lance, 'Turkish' mace (probably of the flanged variety), arming coat or surcoat, *espalier* (probably a padded shoulder defence), what appears to have been an arming cap to support his helmet, a dagger, large and small knives, a caparison for his horse, two shirts, two breeches, two pairs of padded chausses and a narrow belt for his shirt. Other equipment included two small sacks for his nightshirt, arming coat and *espalier* and a leather or coarse sack for his hauberk. Other rules refer to wider sword-belts, with or without buckles, an ordinary hat and probably a

*Sleeping Guards at the Holy Sepulchre, c.1300.* **This carving shows German military styles including an early coat-of-plates, the buckles of which can be seen on the lower figure's back. (***in situ*** 'Easter Shrine' of Cathedral, Constance)**

wide-brimmed felt bonnet. The equipment issued to sergeants was similar though they wore mail *haubergeons*, either short-sleeved or lacking mail mittens; had mail chausses with limited foot protection, perhaps for ease of walking; and war-hats rather than larger helmets. Such war-hats left the face partly exposed but were more suitable in a Middle Eastern climate, as was the 'light equipment' so widely used even by Crusaders newly arrived from the west. 'Old Turkish weapons' are frequently mentioned in the *Rule of the Temple*, suggesting that captured military equipment was, not surprisingly, used by the warriors of the

Carved relief showing an early 12th century Italian warrior. His body armour and mail chausses are shown in different ways. (*in situ* west front of Cathedral, Lucca)

(A) Sword or dagger pommel, probably of Syrian manufacture (Met. Mus., no. 29.152.685, New York). (B) Sword pommel of Peter of Dreux, probably captured at Mansurah in 1250, subsequently purchased in Damascus (Met. Mus., New York). (C–K) Fragments of a coat-of-plates, possibly of a helmet (C) and crossbow bolt-heads, from Castle of Montfort, c. 1270 (Met. Mus., New York). (L–P) Spear- and arrow-heads, plus a work-axe from Athlith castle, late 13th century (Palestine Archaeological Museum, Jerusalem). (Q) Medieval iron arrow-head found near the Yarmouk valley, of a type used by both Saracens and Turcopoles (author's collection).

Crusader States. Such arms and armour was seized at the castle of Harenc by the First Crusade even before the conquest of Jerusalem. Booty following victory generally included useful military equipment, and was clearly re-used by at least the humbler warriors on both sides. The same happened in the 13th century when the Fourth Crusade and its successors in Greece captured vast amounts of armour and weapons from the Byzantines.

Whereas Crusader warriors could be mistaken for Fatimid Egyptian troops early in the 12th century, there were few such confusions in the later 12th and 13th centuries. By that time almost all the Crusaders' foes were either Turks or were equipped in essentially Turkish style. Such arms and armour, particularly under the later 13th century Mamluk dynasty, were quite unlike those used by European warriors.

Weaponry was also manufactured within the Crusader States. Lebanon had long been a vital source of iron for the Middle East and its exploitation made the Lord of Beirut rich. Nearby Acre was a major arms manufacturing centre during the Crusader period, probably using raw materials from Lebanon; while Gaza had made saddles before the Crusader conquest, and Jerusalem continued to be known for its shields during the Crusader occupation. Recent studies also indicate that the area around Ajlun, in what is now the east bank of Jordan, was an important iron mining centre around this time. Though the Crusaders only held the region for a short while, one large valley still bears the name of Wadi Kufranja,

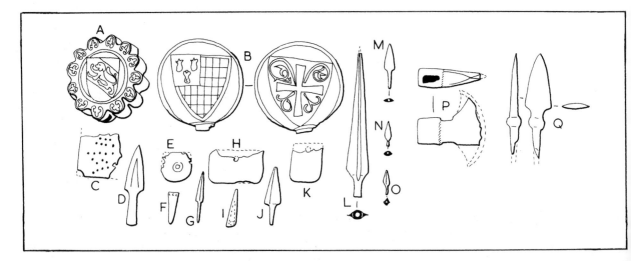

'Valley of the Village of the Franks'. Marash in the north of the County of Edessa was more important as an iron-working region and its early loss must have been a severe blow to the Crusader States. Neighbouring Cilicia was also rich in iron, and though it was ruled by a generally friendly Armenian Kingdom it was rarely under direct Crusader control.

Contrary to popular myth, Crusader armour was no more proof against Turkish arrows than was Byzantine mail. The soldiers described as walking along with so many arrows in their mail hauberks that they looked like porcupines must have been subjected to long-range harassment archery, not direct attack by horse-archers. Middle Eastern and Crusader warriors alike tried to solve the problem by various means, both Fatimids and Franks using 'doubled' mail, which probably meant mail worn in two layers. Other specialised forms of hauberk seen in later Crusades were those with separate mail coifs, and those with only one integral mail mitten protecting the sword-hand. This latter was mentioned in a 13th century Italian Crusader's will and is clearly illustrated in Italian pictorial sources.

A further form of mail armour was of undeniable Middle Eastern origin. This was the *jazerant* or *jazrain* hauberk, a cloth-covered and thickly padded mail garment based upon the earlier Islamic *khazaghand*. Linguistic analysis shows that the term, and probably also the armour, reached Europe via the Turks. It was, however, known in France shortly before the First Crusade, being mentioned in the *Song of Roland*, which suggests that knowledge of the *khazaghand* was brought home by mercenaries

The Mamariye castle at Anamur. Built upon a 3rd century Roman fortress, this castle served the Cilician Armenians and was subsequently extended by the Turkish Karamanoglu dynasty in the 14th century

who had served in Byzantium. The term became more widespread in the 12th century, particularly in epics and romances based upon the Crusades. Surprisingly, perhaps, the corresponding Italian term *ghiazzerina* is not recorded before the early 14th century.

Much more controversial is the possibility of eastern Mediterranean, Byzantine or Islamic influence on the development of rigid or semi-rigid body armours in Europe. These were almost certainly adopted in response to the threat from crossbows or, if the Crusades had any part in the process, from the powerful Middle Eastern composite bow. Some form of body armour was occasionally worn under mail hauberks in late 12th century France. This was the almost certainly hardened leather *cuirie*. Such a technique of construction was popular with various Mediterranean peoples. The true coat-of-plates appeared in Spain, England, France, Germany and Italy in the mid- to late 13th century. It is in the design of this body defence, which was made of relatively small overlapping pieces of metal fastened inside a cloth or leather base, that Byzantine or Islamic influence may perhaps be found. It is worth noting that Mamluk authors mentioned the iron *jawshans* of the Crusaders, the *jawshan* being a lamellar body armour upon which the European coat-of-plates might, to some extent, have been based. Certain terms relating to 'soft' armour also showed

49

unmistakable Islamic influence; the quilted *aketon* coming from the Arabic word *al qutn*—cotton.

Most forms of European helmet used in the Crusader period betrayed no discernible Eastern influence. The preference of all sides for relatively light head defences probably reflected the climate plus, perhaps, a more open and manoeuvrable style of warfare in which good vision was vital. The separate mail coif was known in the Middle East long before Europe and the *bascinet*, which normally had an attached mail aventail rather than being worn over a mail coif, was so similar to long-established oriental forms of helmet that some form of connection seems likely. But this Eastern tradition of helmets was also found in Byzantium, Russia and non-Islamic Central Asia as well as the Muslim world. Recent but as yet unconfirmed reports speak of hardened leather helmets being found in a Crusader castle in Israel, while such leather helmets were certainly known in England by the late 13th century.

Other areas of possible Middle Eastern influence on the development of European military technology include horse-armour. This was probably

unknown in early medieval Europe, but had long been employed by the Byzantines as well as the Egyptian Fatimids and other Muslim armies. One European term for such a protection, *bard*, is widely believed to come from the Arabic *bardha'ah* meaning pack-saddle, though it also has some similarity with the Persian-Turkish-Mamluk terms *bargustuwan*, 'horse-armour', and *bardhanab*, 'crupper' (armour for the rear of a horse). Full mail *bards* were clearly used during the Third Crusade and are mentioned in western Europe around the same time. Quilted horse-armours, which would have been much closer to those used in the Muslim Middle East, appeared in Europe a few years later. So did the *copita* or *chamfron*, a protection for the horse's head; this was the first piece of rigid horse-armour to be used in medieval Europe, but it had long been known in both Central Asia and the Middle East.

The Crusaders and other Europeans were much more reticent when it came to adopting oriental forms of weapon. Only the Byzantines and perhaps Spaniards used the light reed lance-shafts common among Middle Eastern peoples, nor did they readopt the javelin which had virtually died out in most parts of Europe by the late 11th century. The appearance of the dagger as a knightly close-combat weapon in the 13th and 14th centuries probably had more to do with changing tactics and military attitudes within Europe than outside influence, despite the fact that large daggers had always been included in the inventory of a Muslim professional soldier. Some outside influence may have been present in the acceptance of the lighter axe as a knightly weapon, even if only because it was popular among a respected Mamluk foe. The winged mace which appeared in 12th and above all 13th century Europe was, however, clearly of Islamic origin.

\*     \*     \*

## The Crusader Legacy

What, then, were the results of the Crusades? Did they merely embitter relations between Christendom and Islam, or did they make a contribution to the political, cultural or scientific development of either side? And what of those caught in the crossfire—the Christians of the Middle East and the Greek-speaking Byzantines?

Apart from the turmoil and enthusiasm which

they initially caused, the influence of the Crusades on Europe seems to have been marginal. It may prove to be true that returning Crusaders brought back new ideas concerning weapons and even costume. The Middle Eastern *jarid* cavalry javelin-throwing games could have been brought home as a pastime, but not as a serious military exercise. Nor did Turkish horse-archery have any impact on European military prejudices. Various musical instruments, including the warlike *tabor* and *nakker* drums and the more peaceful *oud* (lute) are clearly based on Islamic originals. The drama of the whole Crusading enterprise had a profound effect on literary subject matter, particularly on chivalrous romances of the 12th and 13th centuries, of which the 'Old French Crusade Cycle' is merely the best known example. The subject matter of church sculpture also reflected the Crusading ethos; while Islamic arts, including calligraphy, had a great effect on European minor arts from metalwork, enamels, ivory carving and manuscript decoration to textiles and glass.

The effect of the Crusades on the Middle East was, however, almost entirely negative. Within Islam an earlier attitude of easy tolerance was lost, though the Crusades alone cannot be blamed for this. Societies became more military, more rigid and more conservative even in non-religious matters like scientific enquiry and artistic experiment. The greatest sufferers were, however, those indigenous Christian communities whose churches the Crusades had been designed to 'save' from an infidel yoke. When the First Crusade arrived at the close of the 11th century Syrian, Nestorian, Jacobite, Coptic and Armenian Christians had formed majorities in many parts of what are now Turkey, Iraq, Syria, the Holy Land, Egypt and even the Sudan. The Armenians' story is rather different from the rest, but by the start of the 14th century these communities had either been reduced to local minorities or were in full decline as conversion to Islam gathered pace. Most, though not all, survive to this day but none—not even the Christians of Lebanon—now form a majority within their own country while their cultures are mere shadows of what they had been in earlier times. The Fourth Crusade almost destroyed Byzantium, the greatest Christian power in the eastern Mediterranean; and although Byzantium did regain its capital city, its

***Enemy crushed by the symbolic lion of Modena**, 12th century carved column-base showing a mailed horseman wearing an early form of salet helmet with a nasal. (**in situ** interior of Cathedral, Modena)*

power had been broken and its last long decline was well under way (see MAA 195, *Hungary and the Fall of Eastern Europe*).

The Crusades might have been an epic, but they were also a disaster.

## Further Reading

A. Ben-Ami, *Social Change in a Hostile Environment. The Crusaders Kingdom of Jerusalem* (Princeton 1969)

H. De Curzon, 'La règle de Temple', *Société de l'Histoire de France CCXXVIII* (1886)

G. Dodu, *Histoire des Institutions Monarchiques dans le Royaume de Jérusalem 1099–1291* (reprint New York 1978)

R. Fedden & J. Thomson, *Crusader Castles* (London 1977)

J. C. Marshall, *Warfare in the Latin East 1192–1292* (Ph.D. thesis, London University 1986; a vital supplement to Smail's work dealing with the period up to 1193 and which one hopes will soon be published.)

H. E. Mayer, *The Crusades* (Oxford 1972; perhaps the best single-volume summary of the Crusades.)

J. W. Nesbitt, 'The Rate of March of Crusading Armies in Europe: A Study and Computation,' *Traditio XIX* (1963; a new and interesting approach to medieval military history.)

R. L. Nicholson, *Tancred: A Study of his Career and Work* (Chicago 1940)

D. C. Nicolle, *Arms and Armour of the Crusading Era 1050–1350* (New York 1988; includes a substantial bibliography on arms, armour and warfare during this period.)

The militia of Verona, a 12th century carving showing infantry headed by an armoured standard-bearer (A) and cavalry (B). Their co-operation was probably the model for militias of the 13th century Crusader States. (*in situ* west front of church of San Zeno, Verona)

J. Prawer, *The Crusaders' Kingdom* (New York 1972; specifically concerned with the Kingdom of Jerusalem.)

*Outremer: Studies in the History of the Crusading Kingdom of Jerusalem presented to Joshua Prawer* (Jerusalem 1982; includes articles of military interest.)

J. Richard, *Le Comté de Tripoli sous la Dynastie Toulousaine* (Paris 1945)

J. Richard, *The Latin Kingdom of Jerusalem* (Oxford 1979)

J. Riley-Smith, *The Feudal Nobility and the Kingdom of Jerusalem 1174–1277* (London 1973)

S. Runciman, *A History of the Crusades* (London 1988; re-issued and still the best account of the Crusades as a whole.)

K. M. Setton (edit.), *A History of the Crusades* (Univ. of Wisconsin, 1955, continuing multi-volume anthology of articles including the most recent scholarship.)

R. C. Smail, 'Crusaders' Castles of the Twelfth Century,' *Cambridge Historical Journal X* (1950–52)

R. C. Smail, *The Crusaders in Syria and the Holy Land* (London 1973; Thames & Hudson *Ancient Peoples & Places* series.)

R. C. Smail, *Crusading Warfare 1097–1193* (Cambridge 1956)

Readers with a serious interest in current research into all aspects of Crusader history should consult the annual *Society for the Study of the Crusades and the Latin East Bulletin*.

# The Plates

*A: The Peasants' Crusade*

*A1: French peasant, late 11th century*

Few of the poorest classes accompanied the so-called Peasants' Crusades and they were probably even more inclined to rob than the others, being persistently short of food. Many were armed only with implements like this man's pitch-fork and domestic knife. He also wears a simple cape, a countryman's straw hat and carries a *scrip* (pouch) from his belt. His breeches are laced up and his hose hang loose. (Sources: *The Winchester Psalter c.*1150, Brit. Lib., Ms. Cott. Nero C.IV f.21; *Chronicle of Winchester c.*1135. Corpus Christ. Coll., Ms. 157 p. 382, Oxford.)

*A2: West European Jew, early 12th century*

In most parts of Western Europe the Jewish communities wore distinctive costumes. To some extent this was forced upon them but to a large degree it also reflected their sense of separate identity. Most illustrated sources date from the 12th century or later but written sources indicate that similar styles had been adopted earlier. This man has the conical hat widely worn as a distinctive item of Jewish dress. His partially shaven head and full beard are also characteristic while his large fur cloak may echo East European or even more distant fashions. (Sources: 'Moses with the Tablets of the Law', bronze door 12th C., *in situ* Church of San Zeno, Verona.)

### A3: Knight from Lotharingia, late 11th century

This man is clearly a poor member of the *miles*, or professional warrior class. Yet he still has the basic equipment of his calling: a mail hauberk of an old-fashioned type, a kite-shaped shield and a simple two-piece helmet. His plain, but well made sword was probably manufactured in the Rhineland and his saddle is of the tall kind developed for combat with the couched lance. (Sources: 'Christ Triumphant' *Reliquary of St. Hadelin* 1046, Church of St. Martin, Visé; *St. Etienne Bible* 1109, Bib. Munic., Dijon; font from Tournai, early 12th C., *in situ* Church of Our Lady, Dendermonde; carved reliefs 1130–40, *in situ* exterior of Abbey Church, Andlau.)

### B/C: The First Crusade

Warriors from many parts of western Christendom took part in the First Crusade and, though there was a great deal of uniformity in European military equipment at this time, there were also regional variations. This illustration includes an attempted reconstruction of Jerusalem's Dome of the Rock as it appeared in the late 11th century.

### B/C1 Knight from the County of Toulouse, c.1100

Fluted or ribbed helmets appear in a few southern French sources. Otherwise this man is armed much like those Norman warriors who conquered England half a century earlier. His broad-bladed spear is for fighting on foot while the interior of his shield has two *enarmes* or holding straps plus a shoulder *guige* drawn tight when not in use. (Sources: carved capitals c.1100, *in situ* cloisters, Abbey of St. Peter, Moissac; carved capitals late 11th–early 12th C., *in situ* church, St. Nectaire.)

### B/C2: German warrior from Franconia, c.1100

Although some of the best weapons in Europe were made in the Rhineland, the military aristocracy of this region seems to have been old-fashioned in many aspects of organisation and equipment. For example the large round shield and side-slit mail hauberk both seem designed for infantry combat. (Sources: sword 1100–50, Higgins Armory, Worcester, USA; 'Martyrdom of St. Felix', altarfront c.1100, *in situ* church, Abdingdof; relief carvings c.1135, *in situ* exterior of Abbey Church, Andlau; *Reliquary of St. Candide* early 12th C., Treasury, Abbey of St. Maurice, Switzerland.)

*'Alexander the Great battles King Poros of India'* in a *Histoire Universelle* from Acre, c.1287. Alexander's army includes a mailed infantryman with a small round shield while two of the Indians on the first elephant appear to be throwing incendiary grenades (Bib. Nat., Ms. Fr. 20125, Paris).

Walls of the Blachernae quarter at the northern end of the land-walls of Istanbul where the Fourth Crusade broke into Constantinople. These walls were a medieval addition, strengthening this part of the city's ancient defences.

### B/C3: Norman knight from southern Italy, c.1100

There is evidence that the Normans of southern Italy were militarily more advanced than their cousins in France or England, perhaps reflecting Byzantine or Islamic influence. This man is based on crude but very important carvings in Bari which can be interpreted as showing mail and lamellar (see Elite 9, *The Normans* Plate I-1) or, as here, mail worn beneath a form of scale cuirass. (Sources: Italian sword 11th C., Mus. of Art no. 1977.167.529, Philadelphia; 'Siege of Jerusalem' carvings early 12th C., *in situ* north door Church of San Nicola, Bari: south Italian chessmen 11th C., Cab. des Med., Bib. Nat., Paris.)

### B/C4: Genoese sailor, early 12th century

The role of Italian sailors in the conquest of the Palestinian coast was very important. Their military equipment was almost certainly similar to that of poorer militiamen in other northern Italian cities. This man has a composite bow, a large dagger and a helmet of stitched leather. No such helmets have survived but may appear in carvings which are otherwise difficult to interpret. (Sources: 'De Repositorii', *Encyclopedia of Maurus Hrabanus* 1023, Lib. Ms. 132, p. 363, Monte Casino; wall painting 11th C., *in situ* Church of San Jacopo, Termeno; carvings early-mid 12th C., *in situ* west door Church of San Zeno, Verona.)

*Soldier at the Betrayal* **on a Mosan bronze font c.1110. This typical early 12th century German warrior has a mail coif off his head and has his large shield slung from a guige. (Plaster cast in the V & A Museum, London; original in church of Sant Barthelemy, Liège)**

### B/C5: Northern French knight equipped for combat on foot, c.1100

The Normans and other northern French troops were prepared to fight on foot even in open battle, as well as in sieges. This man has his long cavalry shield slung by its *guige* over his back and he wields an infantry axe whose peculiar spike is based on relatively unusual carvings. His helmet and mail hauberk are, however, virtually unchanged since the days of William the Conqueror. (Sources: sword inscribed INGELRII c.1050–1100, Coll. of R. E. Oakeshott; carved capitals c.1100, *in situ* cloisters, Abbey of St. Peter, Moissac; *Bayeux Tapestry* late 11th cent., Tapestry Mus., Bayeux; *St. Etienne Bible* 1109, Bib. Munic., Dijon; 'Goliath', carved capital c.1120, *in situ* Cathedral, Vezelay.)

## B/C6: Gascon crossbowman, late 11th century

The crossbow seems to have been accepted quite quickly as a war weapon in southern France. The Gascons used it at sea and this man carries an early type of crossbow which lacked a loading stirrup. His buff leather coat is based on an example illustrated in neighbouring Spain and his striped tunic also seems to betray influence from beyond the Pyrenees. (Sources: 'Demon with crossbow' carved capital late 11th C., *in situ* Cathedral, Toulouse; carved figures 12th C., *in situ* west front of former Cathedral, Oloron Ste. Marie; carved capitals *c*.1120, *in situ* Cathedral, Vezelay; carved capitals *c*.1100, *in situ* cloisters, Abbey of St. Peter, Moissac.)

## D: The Crusader States

The military élite of the Crusader States soon adopted regional fashions, as well as employing local troops. Such styles generally reflected the Middle Eastern climate and were sometimes technologically more advanced than those that the First Crusaders had brought with them. But other fashions, such as beards, tended to provoke scorn and even outrage from newly-arrived European Crusaders. These men stand at the entrance to the spectacular Wadi Numayrah which leads up from the Dead Sea to the Kerak plateau.

### D1: Maronite infantry archer, 12th century

The Maronite Christian community of Syria and Lebanon were among the most reliable indigenous troops in the Crusader States. They mostly fought as light infantry archers and were particularly effective in mountainous terrain. This man's costume is purely Middle Eastern and his bow is of the composite construction seen throughout the region. (Sources: *Queen Melisende's Psalter* 1131–43, Brit. Lib., Ms. Eger. 1139 f. 18v, London; carved capitals 12th C., Local Mus., Nazareth & Greek Orthodox Patriarchate, Jerusalem; carved ivory plaque, Fatimid 11th–12th C., Bargello Mus., Florence,; *Kitab al Sufar* 1130–1, Topkapi Lib., Ms. Ahmad III 3493 f.30r, Istanbul.)

### D2: Brother-knight of the Hospitaller Order, mid-12th century

Regulations governing the costume of members of the Military Orders do not seem to have become rigid until the later 12th century and much remains

*Battle of the Buqaia* **in 1163. Wall paintings made shortly after the battle and showing a Crusader army marching out to meet Nur al Din. (***in situ* **ex-Templar church at Cressac, France)**

unclear about their early history. This knight wears the early form of monastic black mantle and has the Order's red swallow-tail pennon on his lance. His armour consists of a one-piece conical helmet, mail *chausses* on his legs and a cloth-covered *jazrain* hauberk. (Sources; ivory cover of *Queen Melisende's Psalter* early 12th C., Brit. Mus., London; *Winchester Psalter* mid-12th C., Brit. Lib., Ms. Cott. Nero C. IV, London; carved capital *c*.1155, *in situ* Church of Notre Dame du Port, Clermont-Ferrand.)

### D3: Crusader from northern Italy, mid-12th century

Individual pilgrims from Europe provided an important, though short-term, source of military manpower for the Crusader States. This knight comes from one of the great north Italian cities and his equipment differs to some extent from that of France or England. His helmet appears to have two vertical ridges near the front, perhaps indicating that this was thicker than the sides or rear. His hauberk is of a lighter form worn over a quilted *gambeson* and his shield is an early example of the flat-topped type. The rope securing him to his saddle is probably shown on a carving in Verona but this idea did not become popular until the 14th century. (Sources: 'Roland and Farugut', carved relief *c*.1138, *in situ* Church of San Zeno, Verona; carved capitals mid-12th C., *in situ* Cathedral, Parma; carved stone candlestick *c*.1170, Church of San Paolo fuori le Mura, Rome; *Bible* from Florence 1125–50, Mus. Dioc., Trento.)

*E: The Third Crusade, 1189–92*

The Third Crusade essentially consisted of three armies: the Germans, the French under King Philip and the Anglo-French under King Richard the Lion-Heart of England. There were almost no differences between the military equipment of the English and French, which consisted of a further development of the mail hauberk, open helmet and large shield which had been in use since the 11th century.

*E1: Richard the Lion-Heart, late 12th century*

Many reconstructions of King Richard's appearance have relied on sources from late in his reign. This figure, however, is based on earlier illustrations showing him in an open-faced, round-topped helmet and carrying a very large kite-shaped shield. This shield may also have borne only two leopards, rather than the three which were to become the badge of English rulers. Here the king also wears a long-sleeved mail hauberk with rudimentary mail mittens which leave his fingers exposed. (Sources: *First Great Seal of Richard I* 1189, Brit. Lib., no. XXXIX.II; *Great Canterbury Psalter* 1180–90, Bib. Nat., Ms. Lat. 8846 f.2v, Paris; *Psalter of St. Louis c.*1200, Univ. Lib., Leiden.)

*E2: French infantry sergeant from Champagne, late 12th century*

Some sergeants were heavily armoured horsemen, others relatively poor foot soldiers. This man is equipped as an infantry spearman and his shield has an iron foot to be thrust into the ground when fighting in fixed ranks. (Sources: knives & sheaths from London, late 12th C., Mus. of London: *La Charité Psalter* late 12th C., Brit. Lib., Harl. 2895 f.51b, London; 'Herod's Guards' stained glass

**'Defeat of Satan's army before Jerusalem,' English *Apocalypse*, *c.*1270, showing typical late 13th century English equipment. (Bod. Lib., Ms. Douce 180 f.88, Oxford)**

window late 12th C., *in situ* Cathedral, Chartres; ivory chess man, French 12th C., Bargello Mus, Florence.)

### E3: Andrew de Chauvigny, late 12th century

De Chauvigny was one of Richard the Lion-Heart's chief lieutenants. Here he wears a full mail hauberk, though still lacking mittens. His large sword-of-war is suspended on a complicated system of straps which held the weapon at a convenient angle when on horseback. His mail coif is worn over a flat-topped arming cap, giving it a square outline to support a flat-topped helm which itself rested on an additional padded squab around the coif. The helmet is not yet the true Great Helm but is an earlier version with a substantial nasal. (Sources: 'Joshua', *Bible* 1160–70, Cath. Lib., f.209, Winchester; carved wooden staff-finial *c.*1200, Mus. of Fine Arts, no. 54.931, Boston; *Life of St. Guthlac c.*1200, Brit. Lib., Harl. Roll Y.6, London; *Peterborough Psalter* 1222, Fitzwilliam Mus., Ms. 12, f.78, Cambridge.)

### F: The German Crusade, 1197

Military equipment in 'the Empire', particularly in Germany, differed in detail to that of neighbouring France. So did the costume of its knightly class. In some respects German arms and armour were more advanced, though the reasons for this are not clear.

Walls of Didimotiho overlooking the Evros River in north-eastern Greece. This medieval citadel was temporarily seized by the German Crusading Emperor Frederick in 1189 and later served as a vital fortress in the short-lived Crusader 'Empire of Romanie'.

The Crusade of 1197 was, however, a failure, with the German armies being seized by unexplained panic on a number of occasions.

### F1: Hartmann von Aue, late 12th century

This German knight was perhaps more famous as a poet than a warrior, though he seems to have served with distinction in the Holy Land. His arms and armour show certain advanced features including a particularly German form of tall round helmet, this example having a small fixed visor. His full mail hauberk has mittens, his small shield is almost triangular and his sword is a much more pointed thrusting weapon. Von Aue's surcoat has fashionable long sleeves, as one would expect a poet to wear, and his horse has a quilted *bard* or *caparison*. A number of these features could betray Eastern influence, but this is more likely to have come from Byzantium, where many Germans served as mercenaries, than the Islamic world. (Sources: sword *c.*1200, Wallace Coll., London; *Jungfrauenspiegel c.*1200, Kestner Mus., Hanover; *Eneide* late-12th/early 13th C., Staatsbib., Ms. Ger. 20282, Berlin; lost tomb of Count of Flanders, Church of St. Bertin, St. Omer; *The Bamberg Rider* statue *c.*1230, *in situ* Cathedral, Bamberg.)

**Second Great Seal of Richard I of England** in which the king wears a flat-topped and crested great helm but has no surcoat over his mail hauberk. (Public Records Office, London)

### F2: German infantry sergeant, c.1200

A number of sources illustrate very heavily armoured infantry in Germany. This man has a strange mail hauberk with two separate eye-holes, again perhaps reflecting east European influence. His sword is a relatively short infantry weapon designed for both cut and thrust. (Sources: side panels of *Reliquary of St. Hadelin* 1150–75, Church of St. Martin, Visé; *Book of Dialogues of St. Gregory* 1170–1200, Bib. Royale, Ms. 9916–9917, f.86, Brussels; *Eneide* late 12th/early 13th C., Staatsbib., Ms. Ger. 20282, Berlin.)

### F3: German archer, c.1200

Germany was one of the few areas where longbows were still used, though only by semi-independent peasantry in isolated areas. A number of sources also portray scale cuirasses. These could by now have been imaginary, though similar armours reappeared early in the 14th century. Small hand-held wooden bucklers were, however, used by infantry in many regions. (Sources: lost *Hortus Deliciarum* manuscript c.1180; *Eneide* late 12th/early 13th C., Staatsbib., Ms. Ger. 20282, Berlin; painted wooden ceiling late 12th C., *in situ* Church of St. Martin, Zillis; carved relief late 12th/early 13th C.,

*in situ* Cathedral, Freiburg-im-Br.; *Liège Psalter* c.1250, Univ. Lib., Ms. 431, f.188v, Liège; *Psalterium B. Elisabeth* mid-13th C., Mus. Arch. Naz., Ms. CXXXVII, f.1v, Cividale.)

### G: The Fourth Crusade

The Fourth Crusade may have been a disaster for Christendom but it brought Italy into even greater contact with Byzantine culture (including Byzantine military technology) after the establishment of Latin states in the Greek heartland. By the 13th century Byzantium had been under both Western and Turkish military influence for many years and this too would have an impact.

### G1: Dandolo, Doge of Venice, 1204

Though old and virtually blind, the Doge (elected Duke) Dandolo of Venice was a effective war-leader who insisted in being in the thick of the fighting. Here he is dressed in an old-fashioned mail hauberk without a surcoat, which still seems to have been common in northern Italy. He has mail chausses inside his shoes and carries a gold-tipped staff of office. His helmet (held by G3) looks like an early form of *salet* and he wears the fur-lined cap which already served as a mark of the Doge's rank. (Sources: sword 13th C., Mus. of Croatian Arch., Split; wall paintings late 12th/early 13th C., *in situ* Crypt of Massenzio, Basilica, Aquileia.)

### G2: Varangian Guardsman, c.1200

The Varangian Guard of the later Byzantine Empire included a variety of nationalities. The English may have been in a majority but Scandinavians and other Baltic peoples also served. Byzantine military equipment was now showing strong Turkish influence, particularly from those nomadic peoples north of the Black Sea who had recently made deep in-roads into Byzantine Balkan territory. This guardsman has an iron lamellar cuirass over a small mail hauberk. His inlaid helmet with its mail *aventail* and his scabbard which is hung from cords are both in an eastern tradition. This would not be adopted in Western Europe until a century later. (Sources: mail hauberk, 12th–13th C., Local Mus., Kazanlik; helmet and scabbard fragments from Moldavia, location unknown, ex-Spinei; *Barlaam and Joasaph* late 12th/early 13th C., Iviron Monastery Lib., Ms. 463, Mt. Athos.)

## G3: Flemish knight, c.1210

Flemings were to play a leading rôle in the short-lived Latin 'Empire of Romanie'. Despite his lack of a surcoat this man is otherwise equipped in a very up-to-date manner. His helmet is an early version of the true Great Helm, his mail hauberk has integral mittens and he carries a shorter shield than had been seen in the 12th century. (Sources: Sword of St. Maurice 1198–1215, Treasury, Kunsthist. Mus., Vienna; lost tomb slab of Nicola III de Rumigny, after Van dun Berg & Roland; tomb slab of the knight Antione, early 13th C., Curtius Mus., Liège; silver Shrine of Charlemagne 1200–7, *in situ* Cathedral, Aachen; *Eneide* late 12th/early 13th C., Staatsbib., Ms. Ger. 20282, Berlin.)

## H: The Battle of Mansoura, 1250

The battle of Mansoura brought to an end the catastrophic Egyptian Crusade of St. Louis and it showed all too clearly how the best of Western Europe's military élite were now out-classed by their Mamluk foes. The lesson was noted but not learned, and similar disasters were to occur in the 14th century when the descendants of these Crusaders met the Ottomans in open battle.

## H1: Peter of Dreux, Duke of Brittany, c.1250

Many leading noblemen lost their lives in the battle of Mansoura, Peter of Dreux suffering a sword cut across his face from which he later died. This suggests that he was wearing a *chapel de fer* war hat, as shown here, rather than a Great Helm. Peter's sword pommel turned up in the Damascus bazaar not many years ago, perhaps having been handed down through the generations as a war souvenir. It is also worth noting the fact that a stained glass window in Chartres shows Peter of Dreux apparently dropping a sword behind his horse. (Sources: pommel of Peter of Dreux's sword, Met. Mus. of New York; *Maciejowski Bible c.1250*, Pierpont Morgan Lib., New York; 'Peter of Dreux' and other knights, stained glass windows mid-13th C., *in situ* clerestory of Cathedral, Chartres.)

## H2: William, Earl of Salisbury, c.1250

Another noble to die at Mansoura was William of Salisbury. He is shown here in a thickly padded arming cap clearly designed to support a Great Helm. His long shield is rather old-fashioned but the raised shoulders of his surcoat suggest a padded garment or shoulder protection beneath. (Sources: effigy of William Longsword mid-13th C., *in situ* Cathedral, Salisbury; *L'Estoire de Seint Aedward le Roi c.1245*, Univ. Lib., Ms. Ee.III.59, f.32v, Cambridge; *Chanson d'Aspremont c.1250*, Brit. Lib., Ms. Lans. 782, f.12v, London; effigy, mid-13th C., *in situ* Temple Church, London and cast in Victoria & Albert Mus., London.)

## H3: Templar sergeant, c.1250

Although the Military Orders did not wear uniforms as such, their military equipment and appearance was relatively standardised. This infantryman or dismounted sergeant has an iron *cervelliere* worn over a padded coif. His mail coif would go over the helmet. The fearsome weapon he carries is clearly illustrated in manuscripts of the time but its name is not known. (Sources: knife & sheath, 13th C., Mus. of London; *Maciejowski Bible c.1250*, Pierpont Morgan Lib., New York.)

**Bronze aquamanile from Lower Saxony 1250–1300 clearly showing the great helm, tall saddle and straight-legged riding position. (Met. Mus., 64.101.1492, New York)**

## I: Cilician Armenia

Cilician or 'Lesser' Armenia was an important regional power during the late 12th and 13th centuries. Its armies were much larger than those of the Crusader States and, until decline set in after the Mongol invasions, were generally able to keep the neighbouring Turks at bay. Cilician Armenia also frequently intervened in the affairs of the Crusader States.

*St. George*, **13th century icon perhaps made in Crusader Greece. The saint has a mail hauberk and a typically European shield. (Byzantine Mus., inv. 89, Athens)**

## I1: Leon II 'The Great' of Armenia, early 13th century

Leon II ruled over the most glorious period in Cilician history. Armenian costume, arms and armour seem to have been a strange mixture of East and West at this time. A carving over the door of Yilanlikale castle, which is believed to represent Leon II, shows him seated cross-legged in Islamic style, with a Turkish double-breasted coat and an almost European form of crown while in his hand he holds a clearly Western form of sword. (Source: relief carving 13th C., *in situ* gate of Yilanlikale castle, Cilicia).

## I2: Armenian heavy cavalryman, 13th century

Although the military élite of Cilician Armenia had been feudalised under influence from Crusader Antioch, their equipment and style of warfare seems to have been closer to that of their Muslim neighbours, particularly the Turks of Anatolia. Military influences were probably two-way, with Byzantium also playing a rôle. (Sources: carved wooden doors from Monastery of Holy Apostles 1134, Mouch, now in Mus. of Armenian Hist., Yerevan; *Gospels* mid- to late-13th C., Matenadaran Ms. 7651 & 979, Yerevan; *Gospels* c.1270, Freer Gall., no. 32–18, Washington; relief carvings from various sites, 13th C., Museum, Etchmiadzin.)

## I3: Archer from Trabzon, 13th century

Infantry archers from the mountainous hinterland of Trabzon (Trebizond) were the most effective forces in the small Byzantine 'Empire of Trebizond'. They used composite bows and are likely to have been similar in other ways to the infantry archers of neighbouring Caucasus regions, both Christian and Muslim. This man also wears a helmet from southern Russia, perhaps imported from the Crimea which formed Trabzon's only 'empire'. (Sources: helmet from Ukraine 12th–13th C., Hermitage, Leningrad; Byzantine silver dish 12th C., ex-Bazilevsky Coll., Hermitage, Leningrad; Armenian *Gospels* 1262, Walters Art Gall., Ms. W539, Baltimore; ceramic bowl from Baylakan, 12th–13th C. and relief carving from Daghestan, 12th–14th C.: Hermitage, Leningrad.)

## J: The Fall of Acre

The fall of Acre to the Mamluks in 1291 marked the effective end of the Crusader States in the Holy

Land. The last garrison was quite large and included many volunteers from Europe and Cyprus. The siege itself was long and bitter, with the enemy using advanced pyrotechnic weapons. The defenders still relied on essentially Western European forms of arms and armour though some local features had also developed, the most obvious being the use of an oval shield in defensive siege warfare.

*J1: Othon de Grandson, late 13th century*

This Swiss knight commanded a small force of English volunteers defending a section of Acre's wall. Here he is equipped in normal but up-to-date Western style including an almost round-topped Great Helm and padded thigh *cuisses* with iron *poleyns* attached. He has also chosen to fight with a heavy falchion instead of a sword and has discarded his cumbersome sword-belt. (Sources: *Histoire Universelle*, Acre *c.*1287, Bib. Nat., Ms. Fr. 20125, Paris; *Histoire Universelle*, Acre 1290–1, Bib. Laur., Ms. Plu. LXI.10, Florence; effigy of Othon de Grandson *c.*1330, *in situ* Cathedral, Lausanne.)

**Citadel of Trebizond (Trabzon) showing the remains of the *Empresses' Room* (left). The 'Empire of Trebizond' was one of the fragmented Byzantine states that emerged from the wreck of the Fourth Crusade.**

*Crusaders massacre Muslims of Antioch* **showing the unusual mixture of oval or round shields with full mail and round-topped great helms, from a *History of Outremer* made in Acre 1290–91. (Bib. Laur., Ms. Plut. LXI.10, f.61, Florence)**

*Possible participant in the Seventh Crusade, mid-13th century stained glass window showing a primitive form of great helm with a fixed visor to protect the face. (in situ Cathedral, Chartres)*

*J2: Infantry sergeant of the Crusader States, late 13th century*

Mercenary infantry recruited from various parts of Europe played an important rôle in the last decades of the Crusader States. This man is equipped in local style though his coat-of-plates probably originated in Germany. His large dagger or small thrusting sword and round buckler would be suitable for fighting in the confined conditions of a siege. (Sources: *Universal History of William of Tyre* late 13th C., Bib. Munic., Ms. 562, Dijon & Bib. Nat., Ms. Fr. 20125, Paris; 'Betrayal' north French carving 1275–1300, Met. Mus of Art, no. 17.120.5, New York; 'Sleeping Guard' 1250–1300, Prov. Mus., Hanover; monumental brass of Sir Brocardus de Charpignie *c*.1270, via Courtauld Inst., London; effigy 1250–1300, *in situ* Abbey, Pershore.)

*J3: Crossbowman of Crusader States, late 13th century*

Crossbowmen formed an even more vital part of the last Crusader garrisons. Many were recruited from Italy and manuscripts painted in Acre near the end of the 13th century show such men in full mail but often without any form of surcoat. This man is also armed with an early form of *basilard* dagger and has a substantial padded *gambeson* beneath his mail. (Sources: *Histoire Universelle c*.1286, Brit. Lib., Ms. Add. 15268, London & Bib. Nat., Ms. Fr. 20125, Paris; *History of Outremer c*.1280, Saltykov-Shchredrin Lib., Ms. Fr. fol.v.IV.5, Leningrad & Bib. Laur., Ms. Plu. LXI.10, Florence.)

### K: The Kingdom of Cyprus

The Kingdom of Cyprus, which emerged after King Richard of England conquered the island during the Third Crusade, long outlived the other Crusader States in the eastern Mediterranean. It maintained the struggle against the Mamluks for decades. Many widows of high birth arrived in Cyprus following the fall of the other Crusader States; and their hands were often sought by those in Western Europe who were eager to make marriage alliances with illustrious dynasties.

*K1: King Henry II of Cyprus, c.1300*

Henry II, one of the Lusignan rulers of Cyprus, is here shown in the rather Italianate armour which seems to have been common in Cyprus. His Great Helm has a large crest made of stuffed leather. His *greaves* are a new feature, in addition to the iron *poleyns* which protect his knees. One unusual feature which could betray either Byzantine or Mamluk influence is the hanging of his sword from a *guige*. (Sources: incised tomb slabs of Lusignan family from Aya Sofia, Famagusta *c*.1300, soon to be in Local Mus., Limassol; *Histoire Universelle* Acre *c*.1287, Bib. Nat., Ms. Fr. 20125, Paris.)

*K2: Widow of the Gibelet family, late 13th century*

The black-robed widows who survived the Fall of the Kingdom of Jerusalem and other Crusader States were a feature of Cyprus for many years. (Sources: coat-of-arms of wife of Renier de Gibelet 1302, *in situ* church at Panaghia Kiti, Cyprus.)

*K3: Italian squire from Florence, c.1300*

This young man represents the new rich of Italy, the sons of families who made their wealth in trade but who had recently entered the nobility. His arms and armour are in the latest style, with a fabric-covered coat-of-plates whose rivet-heads are disguised by *fleurs-de-lys* and decorated leg-armour of hardened leather. Even his mittens have separate fingers. (Sources: carved relief of Guillaume Balnis 1289, *in situ* Convent of the Annunziata, Florence; wall paintings *c*.1288, *in situ* Dante Hall, town museum, San Gimignano.)

*L: Crusader Fortifications*

The mighty castles of Syria and southern Jordan are often regarded as typical Crusader fortifications. In reality they were not, although they do represent the culmination of a long development. Many, perhaps most, Crusader fortifications were much smaller. Others used those dramatic locations which abound in the Middle East, adding little more than a few walls and a gate. Still others used existing caves, both natural and man-made.

*L1: Reconstruction of the 'cave fortress' of the Caves de Suet*
This extraordinary site, now known as 'Ain Habis in northern Jordan, still exists and our illustration merely attempts to add the external walkways and ladders which are believed to have linked its caves. One of the eroded lower caves has also been

**Donor figure of the *Icon of St. Nicholas* from the Crusader Kingdom of Cyprus, *c.*1300. The knight wears typically European equipment but his horse appears only to carry the front part of its caparison or bard. (Mus. of Makarios Foundation, Nicosia)**

restored, as have the gates which seem to have stood at either end of the access path. (After Nicolle)

*L2: Reconstruction of Belvoir Castle*
Overlooking the Jordan valley from its cliff-top site in southern Galilee, this fortress was an early, classic example of the concentric castle. It consists of a square *castrum*, with corner towers within another larger *castrum*, plus an additional tower at one end. (After Ben Dov, Gardiner & Gilbron)

*L3: Early form of counterweight trebuchet*
This weapon was developed from earlier man-powered mangonels in the eastern Mediterranean late in the 12th century. It could be operated by a much smaller team of men than previous weapons and was also much more accurate.

---

**Notes sur les planches en couleur**

**A1** En fait, peu de paysans, dotés d'un équipement modeste, tels que ceux-ci, accompagnèrent la Croisade dite 'des Paysans'; le manque de nourriture réduisit

**Farbtafeln**

**A1** Tatsächlich haben nur wenige dieser schlicht ausgerüsteten Bauern am sogenannten 'Bauernkreuzzug' teilgenommen; die meisten sind rasch verhungert.

rapidement leurs rangs. **A2** La plupart des communautés juives d'Europe de l'Ouest portaient un costume distinctif, d'une part car la loi l'imposait et d'autre par choix personnel. **A3** Un soldat professionnel impécunieux.

**B/C1** D'après des documents français il y aurait eu des casques à cannelures ou à nervures. La large pointe de lance sert en combat d'infanterie. **B/C2** Les pays rhénans produisirent de fines armes, mais les aristocrates franconiens ont un air désuet dans leur accoutrement, à savoir le casque rond et le haubert fendu sur le côté. **B/C3** L'équipement des Normands du sud de l'Italie présentait une influence orientale contemporaine. **B/C4** Parmi la vêture la plus simple, probablement similaire à celle des milices des cités italiennes septentrionales, voici un casque qui semble être en cuir. **B/C5** Equipé pour combattre à pied, il porte une hache d'un genre qui ne se voit que sur quelques gravures de cette époque. **B/C6** Le manteau de cuir et la tunique rayée révèlent une influence qui pourrait être espagnole. Les Gascons furent les premiers à s'enthousiasmer pour l'arbalète, ils l'utilisaient aussi bien à terre qu'en mer.

**D1** Efficaces et d'une grande loyauté les archers maronites portaient uniquement le costume oriental. **D2** Les réglementations de tenue pour les Ordonnances militaires n'avaient pas encore la rigidité que l'on connaîtra plus tard dans le siècle. **D3** La face du casque a strie, probablement rembourré est une caractéristique du nord de l'Italie; léger haubert sur gambeson rembourré; et casque plat. Notez la corde qui le retient à sa selle, utilisée couramment deux siècles plus tard mais déjà illustrée sur une sculpture du 12ème siècle à Vérone.

**E1** D'après un document plus antérieur du règne de ce roi que les sources normalement utilisées lors des essais de reconstitution; notez le casque ouvert, au sommet arrondi et seulement deux léopards sur le bouclier très large. **E2** Ce sergent d'infanterie relativement pauvre possède un bouclier muni d'un 'pied' en fer qu'il pouvait enfoncer dans le sol lorsqu'il combattait à rangs serrés. **E3** L'un des lieutenants de Richard Coeur de Lion, son épée est suspendue par des bandoulières complexes à un angle pratique pour combattre à cheval. L'on portait un bonnet plat rembourré, qu'est venue remplacer une coif à mailles, rembourrée et supportant le casque plat qui se posait au-dessus.

**F1** Chevalier et poète, il porte de longues manches à la mode. Notez la forme du casque particulièrement germanique, un bouclier presque triangulaire et une épée pointue, arme d'estoc, des caractéristiques en avance sur leur temps. **F2** D'après l'épaisse bourre de la coiffe d'arme et sous le surcot, l'infanterie allemande aurait été lourdement armée, avec ici un haubert peu commun pourvu de deux trous pour les yeux. **F3** De tels arcs ne se voyaient que parmi les paysans dans les endroits isolés; les sources font état de cuirasses à écailles, sans que l'on sache si elles étaient courantes; toutefois les écus de bois étaient fréquents parmi les fantassins européens, pauvres.

**G1** Cet ancien Doge est vêtu d'une chemise de mailles démodée; son casque que porte G3, semble être un des premiers salets cependant. La coiffe à parure de fourrure marque son rang, comme le bâton à pointe dorée. **G2** Un siècle avant celles d'occident, les troupes byzantines avaient adopté des styles turcs tels que casques avec capuchon de mailles, l'aventail, accroché au bas du casque et épées suspendues à des cordons. **G3** Hormis l'absence du surcot, ce Flamand possède un équipement moderne; une forme primitive du grand heaume, l'haubert est intégral avec mitaines tandis que le bouclier est raccourci.

**H1** Le fait que Pierre de Dreux fut frappé fatalement d'un coup d'épée au visage, à Mansoura, laisse penser qu'il portait un chapel-de-fer. Il est remarquable que l'on ait identifié récemment le pommeau de son épée dans un bazar de Damas. **H2** Notez l'épaisse bourre de la coiffe d'arme et sous le surcot; toutefois ce long bouclier est plutôt démodé. **H3** Fantassin ou sergent à pied portant une cervelière sur une coif rembourrée; la coiffe à mailles se portait sur le casque. Cette arme est clairement présentée dans les manuscrits sans que l'on en sache le nom.

**I1** Un mélange étrange, présenté sur une gravure, avec costume oriental et pièces occidentales, une bigarrure caractéristique des Arméniens qui se trouvaient au croisement de deux cultures. **I2** Les influences byzantine et turque d'Anatolie sont toutes deux reconnaissables dans l'équipement arménien et le style de guerre. **I3** Notez le casque du sud de la Russie porté par cet efficace archer caucasien de l'enclave byzantine de Trebizond.

**J1** Commandant suisse d'une unité anglaise sur les murs d'Acre, il porte un grand heaume presque rond, des cuisses garnies de bourre avec poleyns de fer. **J2** Equipement de style local hormis la cotte à plates, d'origine germanique probablement. **J3** Des manuscrits d'Acre décrivent ces arbalétriers au rôle vital, souvent italiens, entièrement couverts de mailles.

**K1** Cette armure italianisée semble avoir été courante à Chypre; la crête du grand heaume est en cuir bourré; notez les greaves, un nouvel élément. **K2** Des veuves en robes noires venues de terre sainte, saisie par l'ennemi, furent une caractéristique de l'Ile pendant de nombreuses années. **K3** Les tout derniers styles d'armures arborés par l'une des catégories d'anciens marchands italiens nouvellement ennoblis.

**L1** Tentative de reconstruction extérieure de l'extraordinaire fortification de grotte, encore visible à Ain Habis, en Jordanie du nord. **L2** Exemple classique des premiers châteaux concentriques, sur une falaise au sud de la Galilée. **L3** L'un des premiers trébuchets à bascule, mis au point à partir d'un mangonneau à la fin du 12ème siècle; il était beaucoup plus précis et nécessitait une équipe moins nombreuse.

**A2** Die meisten westeuropäischen Judengemeinschaften trugen auffallende Kleidung—teils aufgrund gesetzlicher Bestimmungen, teils nach eigener Wahl. **A3** Ein mittelloser Berufssoldat.

**B/C1** Gekehlte oder geriffelte Helme sind aus einigen südfranzösischen Quellen bekannt. Die breite Speerspitze dient dem Kampf im Fussvolk. **B/C2** Im Rheinland entstanden ausgezeichnete Waffen, aber die fränkischen Aristokraten sehen mit ihrer Ausrüstung altmodisch aus—siehe den Rundschild und die seitlich geschlitzte Halsberge. **B/C3** Die Normannen in Süditalien zeigten bei ihrer Kampfausrüstung die letzten östlichen Einflüsse. **B/C4** Zu den simplen Ausrüstungsstücken—wahrscheinlich ähnlich denen der armen norditalienischen Stadtmilizen—gehört ein Helm, den wir für Leder halten. **B/C5** Für den kampf zu Fuss ausgerüstet, trägt er eine Axt, wie man sie nur aus einigen Schnitzereien aus dieser zeit kennt. **B/C6** In diesem Büffelledermantel und dem gestreiften Wams ist wahrscheinlich spanischer Einfluss zu erkennen. Die Gascogner waren schon früh begeisterte Armbrustschützen und verwendeten diese Waffe zu Lande wie auf See.

**D1** Die tüchtigen und treuen Maroniter Bogenschützen trugen ausschiesslich östliche Kleidung. **D2** Bekleidungsvorschriften für die Militärordern waren noch nicht so streng wie später in dem Jahrhundert. **D3** Zu den norditalienischen Merkmalen gehört die Erhebung an der wahrscheinlich verstärkten Helmvorderseite, die leichte Halsberge über dem gepolsterten Gambeson und der flache Schild. Er ist durch ein Seil mit dem Sattel verbunden—allgemein üblich zwei Jahrhunderte später, aber schon in einer veronesischen Schnitzerei aus dem 12. Jhdt. zu sehen.

**E1** Aus einer früheren Quelle in der Regierungszeit des Königs als jene, die sonst für Rekonstruktionsversuche benutzt werden; siehe offenen, rundem helm, und nur 2 Leoparden auf einem sehr grossen Schild. **E2** Dieser relativ arme Infanteriesergeant hat einen Schild mit einem eisernen 'Fuss', der bei Kämpfen in einer eng geschlossenen Einheit in den Boden eingedrückt wird. **E3** Einer der Leutnants von Richard Löwenherz—sein Schwert ist durch komplexe Bindungen im geeigneten Winkel für den Einsatz zu Pferd eingerichtet. Eine gepolsterte flache Kappe wurde getragen, dazu ein Panzer-Coif mit Polsterung für den flachen Helm, der seinerseits auf einem gepolsterten Kissen um den Coif ruhte.

**F1** Dieser Ritter und Dichter trägt moderne, lange Ärmel. Siehe die typisch deutsche Helmform, den fast dreieckigen Schild und das spitze Stechschwert—alles moderne Merkmale. **F2** Abbildungen in Quellen zeigen die deutsche Infanterie als schwer bewaffnet—hier mit einer seltsamen Halsberge mit Augenlöchern. **F3** Solche Bogen waren jetzt nur bei Bauern in abgelegenen Gebieten zu sehen; man sieht Abbildungen von Schuppenpanzern, doch weiss man nicht, wie verbreitet das war; hölzerne Buckelschilde waren aber unter den armen europäischen Fusssoldaten allgemein verbreitet.

**G1** Der alte Doge trägt eine altmodische Rüstung, doch sein Helm, auch von G3 getragen, scheint ein früher Salet zu sein. Die pelzbesetzte Kappe ist Abzeichen seines Ranges ebenso wie der Stab mit Goldknauf. **G2** Ein Jahrhundert vor dem Westen rungen die Truppen von Byzanz türkische Merkmale wie Helme mit Panzer-Aventail und an Schnüren hängende Schwerter. **G3** Abgesehen vom fehlenden Wappenrock trägt dieser Flame moderne Ausrüstung: eine frühe Form des grossen Helms, Halsberge mit angeschlossenen Fäustlingen und verkürzter Schild.

**H1** Die Tatsache, dass Peter von Dreux einen tödlichen Schwertstreich quer übers Gesicht erhielt—in der Schlacht von Mansoura—deutet an, dass er ein Chapel-de-Fer trug. Interessanterweise wurde der Knauf seines Schwertes vor kurzem in einem Bazar in Damaskus entdeckt. **H2** Siehe dick gepolsterte Kappe, und Wappenrock; der lange Schild hingegen ist eher altmodisch. **H3** Infanterist oder abgesessener Sergeant mit Cervelliere über gepolstertem Coif; das gepanzerte Coif würde über dem Helm getragen. Die Waffe ist in Manuskripten deutlich zu erkennen, doch ist ihr Name unbekannt.

**I1** Eine Schnitzerei zeigt diese seltsame Mischung östlicher Kleidung mit westlichen Stücken, typisch für die Armenier am Kreuzweg zweier Kulturen. **I2** Anatolisch-türkische und byzantinische Einflüsse sind bei armenischer Asurüstung und Kriegführung erkannbar. **I3** Sie südrussischen Helm dieses sehr wirksamen kaukasischen Bogenschützen aus der byzantinischen Enklave von Trebizond (Trapezunt).

**J1** Der Schweizer Kommandant einer englischen Einheit auf den Mauern von Acre; er trägt einen fast undköpflige grossen helm und gepolsterte Cuisses mit eisernen Poleyns. **J2** Lokale Ausrüstung, abgesehen von dem Plattenpanzer—wahrscheinlich aus Deutschland. **J3** Manuskripte aus Acre zeigen die sehr wichtigen Armbrustschützen, meist Italiener, in voller Rüstung.

**K1** Rüstungen italienischen Stils scheinen auf Zypern alltäglich gewesen zu sein; der Kamm der grossen Helms besteht aus ausgestopftem Leder; siehe Greaves (Beinschienen), damals eine Neuheit. **K2** Schwarzgekleidete Witwen aus dem verlorenen Heiligen Land waren viele Jahre lang ein vertrauter Anblick auf der Insel. **K3** Die neuesten Arten von Rüstungen werden von Angehörigen der neu geadelten Kaufmannsklasse Italiens getragen.

**L1** Versuch einer äusserlichen Rekonstruktion der aussergewöhnlichen Höhlenfestung bei Ain Habis in Nordjordanien. **L2** Frühe Form eines Trebuchet mit Gegengewichten, entwickelt, und zwar aus dem handbetriebenen Mangonel des späten 12. Jahrhunderts; es war wesentlich genauer und benötigte weniger Besatzung.